LE CORDON BLEU

QUICK
CLASSICS

LE CORDON BLEU

QUICK CLASSICS

JENI WRIGHT &
LE CORDON BLEU CHEFS

MACMILLAN CANADA
TORONTO

A CASSELL BOOK

This book first published 1998 by Cassell Plc, Wellington House, 125 Strand, London WC2R 0BB

First published in Canada in 1998 by Macmillan Canada

1 2 3 4 5 Cassell 02 01 00 99 98

Canadian Cataloguing in Publication Data

Wright, Jeni
Le Cordon Bleu quick classics: sophisticated food in no time at all

Includes index.
ISBN 0-7715-7626-9

1. Quick and easy cookery. I. Title.

TX833.5.W74 1998   641.5'55   C98-931212-7

This book is available at special discounts for bulk purchases by your group for sales promotions, premiums, fundraising and seminars. For details, contact: Macmillan Canada, Special Sales Department, 29 Birch Avenue, Toronto, ON M4V 1E2. Tel: 416-963-8830.

Le Cordon Bleu and the publishers would like to express their gratitude to the following people:

LONDON	PARIS
Susan Eckstein	Chef Gregory Steneck
Chef Neil Paton	Katharyn Shaw
Helen Barnard	Aliette Saman
Alison Welfare	

Notes

Follow one set of measurements only, either metric or imperial

All spoon measurements are level

1 tablespoon = 15 ml

1 teaspoon = 5 ml

Cover and text design by Richard Carr
Edited by Jenni Fleetwood
Photographs by Amanda Heywood
Home Economist Carole Handslip

Printed and bound in Italy by Graphicom

CONTENTS

Foreword

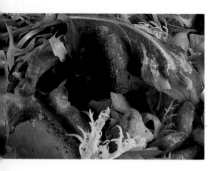

THE ESSENCE OF *Le Cordon Bleu Quick Classics* is the combining of fresh and light produce with top-quality ready made foods to produce imaginative dishes in as little time as possible. All of the recipes are based on classic French culinary techniques, while contemporary kitchen aids and clever shortcuts ensure preparation and cooking times are kept to a minimum. *Le Cordon Bleu Quick Classics* will be your guide and inspiration in the art of dining and entertaining, so you can enjoy the pleasure of a delicious homemade meal around your own table, whether you are eating on your own after a hard day's work or relaxing with your family and friends at the weekend.

First Courses range from soups to salads and seafood, and many of the recipes can double up as light lunches or suppers. The dishes in the After Work chapter have been chosen for their fast and easy preparation, and are made with ingredients you can buy easily on your way home from work or may already have in your store-cupboard, refrigerator or freezer. They range from hearty soups and warm salads to pasta, risotto, fish and steak. In Weekend Entertaining there are sophisticated recipes for special occasions. Some of these may take more time than others, but there are chef's tips on preparing ahead and a special feature on menu planning – both will help you entertain with ease. The chapter on Vegetables, Salads & Accompaniments has ideas for simple vegetable dishes and imaginative international recipes, while in the Desserts chapter you will find a choice of nursery puddings and both simple and special occasion desserts. Whatever you choose, it will be mouthwateringly delicious. At the end of the book there is an invaluable chapter on basics – a storecupboard checklist to help streamline your shopping, then recipes for simple preparations you may want to make should you choose not to use ready prepared foods.

Le Cordon Bleu has over a century of experience in culinary education with five schools world-wide, in France, Great Britain, Japan, Australia and North America. It has a highly esteemed reputation among both professional and amateur chefs with, 32 permanent master chefs teaching a student body made up of 50 different nationalities. The world-wide reputation of Le Cordon Bleu was proven in 1996 when the school was chosen by the Shanghai Tourist Authority to train the first Chinese chefs sent abroad to learn Western culinary techniques.

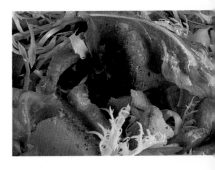

Motivated students are drawn to Le Cordon Bleu from all walks of life. Those with either professional aspirations or a keen interest in fine cooking benefit immensely from a Le Cordon Bleu education. The name evokes images of quality, tradition and unerring commitment to excellence at every level. This is increasingly true as Le Cordon Bleu enters its second century and recognizes a modern world of ever-changing lifestyles.

Le Cordon Bleu Quick Classics brings Le Cordon Bleu and the expertise of its chefs to your kitchen. The recipes are quick, delicious and prepared with a minimum of fuss, leaving you time to explore even more creative possibilities of your own. *Le Cordon Bleu Quick Classics* has been compiled with this in mind, knowing that superb food can be prepared quickly with minimum effort for maximum effect, without compromising flavour and excellence.

First Courses

FIRST COURSES are generally only served for special occasions, so they need to be really good. First impressions count.

Without doubt, the best first courses are those that can be prepared in advance. This will leave you free to be with your guests when they arrive, and to concentrate on things like vegetables, most of which need to be freshly cooked just before serving.

If you are short of time, you will often be so busy thinking of what you will cook for the main course that the first course will be forgotten until the last minute. So take care to plan the whole meal together, to get the balance right, not only in terms of flavours and richness, but also from the timing point of view. If you are planning to serve meat for the main course, choose a fish or vegetable first course; if fish is the main course, choose meat or vegetables to start. Read through the list of ingredients in each recipe and make sure not to serve similar flavours or cream in every course. By the same token, take care not to serve a strongly flavoured starter followed by a delicate main course.

In this chapter you will find that all of the dishes require a minimum of time and trouble. Some of them can be made the day before and left in the refrigerator overnight. When entertaining, it helps enormously to lay the table several hours in advance – if not the day before – and to have the first course set out on the table before people arrive, together with any accompaniments like bread or rolls and butter. Then all you have to do is uncover the food just before you invite your guests to sit down.

Remember above all that the first course is only a taste of things to come. Serve small portions to whet the appetite and leave your guests looking forward to the rest of the meal.

Courgette and Roasted Garlic Soup

Serves 4

Preparation time: 15 minutes

Cooking time:
about 35 minutes

Chef's Tips

If you don't want to go to the trouble of roasting your own garlic, then removing the flesh from the skins, buy a jar of roasted garlic paste and keep it in the refrigerator. It is immensely versatile for adding an instant smoky garlic flavour to sauces, soups and casseroles. For this recipe you will need about 2-3 tablespoons.

Variation

If you prefer a smoother finish, work the soup through a sieve after puréeing.

THIS IS A richly flavoured soup that can be served hot or cold. It goes especially well with warm focaccia, either plain or flavoured with onion or herbs. Serve it in summer or autumn when courgettes are most plentiful.

500 g (1 lb) courgettes
3 tablespoons olive oil
900 ml (1½ pints) hot vegetable stock
salt and freshly ground black pepper
flesh from 1 small head of Roasted Garlic (page 184)
200 ml (7 fl oz) double cream

1 Trim and slice the courgettes. In a large saucepan, heat the olive oil over moderate heat. Add the courgettes and cook, stirring occasionally, for 15 minutes or until they are soft.

2 Pour in the stock, season to taste and bring to the boil. Cover and simmer for about 20 minutes until the courgettes are very soft and falling apart.

3 Pour the soup into a food processor or blender, add the roasted garlic flesh and purée until smooth. If serving hot, return to the pan, add about three-quarters of the cream and heat through. If serving cold, pour into a bowl and allow to cool, then stir in three-quarters of the cream, cover and refrigerate for at least 4 hours or overnight.

To Serve Pour into a soup tureen or individual bowls and swirl the remaining cream in the centre of the soup.

FRESH TOMATO AND PEPPER SOUP WITH BASIL

A BRIGHTLY COLOURED SOUP for late summer when peppers and tomatoes are plentiful, ripe and full of flavour. Although it is served hot here, it is equally good chilled for a sunny al fresco meal.

2 red peppers
500 g (1 lb) tomatoes, preferably Italian plum
1 small onion
1 garlic clove
2 tablespoons olive oil
800 ml (1⅓ pints) hot vegetable stock
good pinch of sugar
salt and freshly ground black pepper
fresh basil leaves, to serve

Serves 4

Preparation time: 10 minutes

Cooking time:
about 30 minutes

1   Roughly chop the peppers and tomatoes. Finely chop the onion and garlic, keeping all the vegetables separate.

2   In a large saucepan, heat the olive oil over low heat. Add the onion and stir for 2 minutes without colouring, then add the peppers and cook for 5 minutes. Add the tomatoes and garlic, cook for 10 minutes, then pour in the stock. Add the sugar and seasoning to taste. Bring to the boil, cover and simmer over moderate heat for 10 minutes.

3   Purée the soup in a food processor or blender until smooth, then strain through a fine sieve back into the pan. Bring to the boil, then lower the heat and adjust the seasoning to taste if necessary.

To Serve   Pour into a soup tureen or individual bowls. Quickly shred the basil and sprinkle over the soup just before serving.

Variations

If you have a jar of pesto in the refrigerator, try adding a spoonful or two to the soup before puréeing. This is an especially good idea if you think the tomatoes might lack flavour. Red pesto will deepen the colour of the soup, green pesto will tone it down.

For a rich, smoky flavour, use 2 chopped roasted red peppers instead of fresh peppers. You can buy them loose or in jars, or roast your own (page 184). Add them to the soup with the tomatoes in step 2.

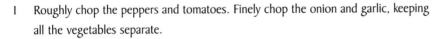

CUCUMBER AND DILL SOUP

THIS ICE-COLD Scandinavian-inspired soup is delicious with delicate, wafer-thin Swedish crispbread. It is the perfect first course for a barbecue party. Serve in chilled bowls – white really shows up the glorious green colour.

1½ large cucumbers
1 small handful of fresh mint
1 small handful of fresh dill
500 ml (16 fl oz) cold chicken or vegetable stock
150 ml (¼ pint) natural yogurt
salt and freshly ground black pepper

To Serve

4 tablespoons natural yogurt
fresh dill and/or mint sprigs

1   Trim the ends off the cucumber and discard, then chop the cucumber into chunks and place in a food processor fitted with the metal blade. Add the mint and dill. Process until finely chopped, then add the stock through the feeder tube and process again until well mixed.

2   Strain the soup through a fine sieve into a bowl, then gradually whisk in the yogurt until evenly blended. Season to taste with salt and pepper.

3   Cover and refrigerate for at least 4 hours.

To Serve   Whisk the soup well and taste for seasoning. Pour into individual soup bowls, swirl a spoonful of yogurt in the centre of each and garnish with mint and/or dill.

Serves 4

Preparation time: 20 minutes

Chef's Tip

Prepare the soup the day before, cover the bowl tightly with cling film and keep in the refrigerator overnight. Put the tureen or soup bowls in the refrigerator at the same time so they will be chilled as well.

PRAWN AND GINGER SOUP

Serves 4

Preparation time: 15 minutes

**Cooking time:
about 25 minutes**

Chef's Tip

*Raw prawns are grey – they
only turn their more familiar
pink colour when they are
cooked. They are relatively
easy to buy fresh or frozen at
fishmongers or supermarkets
with fresh fish counters, and
you can use either for this
soup. To remove the black
intestinal veins, slit the prawns
down their backs and ease
out the veins with the point of
the knife. Cooked prawns can
also be used, but only heat
them through for 1 minute or
they may become tough and
chewy.*

A FUSION OF ORIENTAL and French cuisines takes place in this fresh-tasting soup.
The ginger makes it spicy hot, while the herbs have a cooling effect. Serve
with crisp prawn crackers.

2 medium celery sticks
1 garlic clove
30 g (1 oz) fresh root ginger
8–12 raw prawns in their shells
1 lemon grass stalk
2 star anise
15 g (½ oz) fresh dill sprigs
500 ml (16 fl oz) canned chicken consommé or chicken stock
salt and freshly ground black pepper
a few fresh chives or basil sprigs
1 egg white, to serve

1   Roughly chop the celery and garlic and half the ginger and put them in a saucepan.
    Shell the prawns, and add the heads and shells to the pan. Bruise the lemon grass
    by smashing it with a pestle or the end of a rolling pin, then add to the pan with the
    star anise and dill stalks.

2   Pour in the consommé or stock and 250 ml (8 fl oz) water. Season with salt and
    pepper. Bring to the boil, then lower the heat, cover and simmer for 20 minutes.

3   Halve the prawns lengthways and remove any black intestinal veins. Cut the remaining
    ginger into very fine, needle-like threads. Chop the dill leaves and snip the chives
    or basil with scissors.

4   Strain the liquid and discard the solids. Return the liquid to the rinsed pan, add
    250 ml (8 fl oz) water and bring to the boil. Lower the heat, add the prawns,
    ginger threads and herbs and simmer gently for 3 minutes. Taste for seasoning.

To Serve   Lightly beat the egg white with a fork to loosen it without letting it
become frothy, then pour it into the hot soup and stir it constantly to create fine
threads. Pour the soup into warm bowls and serve immediately.

MIXED GREENS WITH GOAT'S CHEESE TOASTS

F OR VARIETY OF flavour, shape and texture, buy a bag of mixed greens from the supermarket. Good combinations are frisée, herbs, lamb's lettuce and rocket, sometimes labelled 'continental salad'.

30 g (1 oz) pine nuts
12 slices of baguette
3 crottins de Chavignol
125 g (4 oz) mixed greens

Dressing

2 tablespoons red wine vinegar or raspberry vinegar
salt and freshly ground black pepper
8 tablespoons olive oil

Serves 4

Preparation time: 15 minutes

Cooking time: 3-5 minutes

1   Lightly toast the pine nuts under a hot grill. Toast the baguette until light golden on both sides. Slice each crottin into 4 discs and place 1 disc on each slice of toasted baguette. Leave the grill on.

2   Make the dressing: whisk the vinegar with salt and pepper to taste, then whisk in the oil. Toss with the mixed greens and divide between 4 plates.

3   Place the crottin toasts on a baking sheet and put under the hot grill for 3-5 minutes until the cheese is golden brown and bubbling.

To Serve   Arrange the goat's cheese toasts on the salad and sprinkle the toasted pine nuts over the top. Serve immediately.

Chef's Tip

French crottins de Chavignol are sold at supermarkets and delicatessens. They are medium-fat, hard goat's cheeses that are small and round, the perfect size and shape for cutting into discs for grilling. If you can't get them, buy a log of goat's cheese and slice it into rounds about 1.25 cm (½ inch) thick.

SMOKED DUCK WITH BROCCOLI AND ALMONDS

I F YOU LEAVE the glazed skin and fat on the smoked duck it will look attractive, but if you prefer to cut fat and calories, simply strip it off with your fingers before slicing the breast into thin strips.

250 g (8 oz) broccoli florets

salt and freshly ground black pepper

30 g (1 oz) flaked almonds

1 smoked duck breast, weighing about 300 g (10 oz)

Dressing

3 tablespoons cider vinegar or red wine vinegar

5 tablespoons hazelnut oil

5 tablespoons sunflower oil

Serves 4

Preparation time:
15-20 minutes

1   Divide the broccoli into tiny sprigs and trim the stalks. Blanch the sprigs in salted boiling water for 1 minute, drain and refresh immediately under cold running water. Drain again and leave to dry on kitchen paper.

2   Put the almonds in a non-stick frying pan and toss over moderate heat for about 3 minutes until evenly toasted. Turn into a bowl and set aside to cool.

3   Make the dressing. Put the vinegar in a large bowl, add salt and pepper to taste, then whisk in the oils. Add the broccoli and toss well to coat in the dressing. Set aside for at least 30 minutes.

4   Cut the smoked duck on the diagonal into thin slices.

To Serve   Arrange the duck on individual plates, overlapping the slices slightly. Toss the almonds with the broccoli and spoon next to the duck. Drizzle any dressing from the bottom of the bowl over the broccoli, or over the duck if you prefer, and grind black pepper over the top.

Chef's Tips

Whole smoked duck breasts, usually imported from France, are sold at supermarkets, delicatessens, some butchers and gourmet food shops, or you can buy them ready sliced. Whole smoked chicken breasts are also available, and can be used in this recipe. They are smaller than duck breasts, so you will need 2 to serve 4 people.

You can prepare this dish the night before. Toss the broccoli in the dressing and cover the bowl with cling film. Slice the duck, arrange on plates and cover with cling film. Just before serving, add the almonds and spoon the broccoli next to the duck.

FILO PURSES OF FISH

Serves 6

Preparation time: 20 minutes

Cooking time: 10 minutes

Chef's Tips

Ready made filo pastry is available frozen in boxes from the freezer cabinets of most supermarkets. Be careful to handle it gently because it is paper thin, and keep it covered with a damp cloth until it is buttered or it may dry out and crack. In this recipe you will be left with quite a few trimmings; refreeze them to use on top of a pie at a later date.

For an oriental flavour, use cod or monkfish instead of salmon, with 1 teaspoon mango chutney and 2 teaspoons chopped fresh coriander in place of the dill.

THESE CRISP LITTLE pastries have a classic Scandinavian filling of salmon, lemon and dill. They look and taste delicate, and are very good with a crisp, dry white wine. They can be prepared in advance and baked at the last moment.

300 g (10 oz) salmon fillet, skinned
finely grated rind of 1 lemon
1 tablespoon chopped fresh dill
salt and freshly ground black pepper
1 x 275 g packet frozen filo pastry sheets, thawed
about 100 g (3½ oz) butter, melted and cooled
150 ml (¼ pint) crème fraîche
fresh dill sprigs, to garnish

1 Preheat the oven to 220°C (425°F) Gas 7. Cut the fish into 18 chunks and place them in a bowl. Add the lemon rind, dill, ½ teaspoon salt and plenty of pepper. Toss well to mix.

2 Cut the stack of filo sheets into a 15 cm (6 inch) square. Lay 1 sheet on a board and brush with melted butter. Lay another sheet on top and brush this with more butter. Place 3 pieces of fish in the centre of the square; top with ½-1 teaspoon crème fraîche.

3 Gather up the edges of the filo to form a purse, squeeze just above the filling, then twist once to create a drawstring effect. Place on a baking sheet and brush gently with a little more butter. Repeat to make 5 more purses. Bake for 10 minutes.

To Serve Place the purses on individual plates with a spoonful of the remaining crème fraîche alongside, topped with a sprig of feathery dill. Serve immediately.

LAYERED VEGETABLE TERRINE

S TUDDED WITH ROWS of colourful vegetables, this chilled terrine is light, fresh and colourful. Serve it in summer when vegetables are at their best. Crusty French bread or ciabatta makes a good accompaniment.

a little olive oil
1 medium carrot, about 90 g (3 oz)
1 small courgette, about 100 g (3½ oz)
90 g (3 oz) trimmed French beans
125 g (4 oz) spinach leaves, any thick stalks removed
90 g (3 oz) baby sweetcorn
salt and freshly ground black pepper
1 x 12 g sachet powdered gelatine
400 ml (14 fl oz) tomato juice
1–2 teaspoons Worcestershire sauce, to taste
1 packet fresh basil leaves

Serves 6-10

Preparation time: 1 hour,
plus at least 4 hours
to chill the terrine

1   Brush a 23 x 12.5 cm (9 x 5 inch) loaf tin with oil, then line with cling film, letting it overhang the sides. Brush the film with a little oil. Peel the carrot and cut it into matchsticks. Cut the courgette into very thin rounds.

2   Cook each type of fresh vegetable separately in a saucepan of salted boiling water until just tender. Allow 2 minutes for each, except the sweetcorn, which needs about 6 minutes. As each type is cooked, rinse under cold running water, then spread out on a tea towel to dry. Cut the sweetcorn in half lengthways.

3   Sprinkle the gelatine over the tomato juice in a small pan. Leave until clear, then gently warm through, stirring to dissolve the gelatine. Add Worcestershire sauce and seasoning to taste and let cool to room temperature.

4   Line the tin with three-quarters of the spinach. Finely shred the basil. Layer the vegetables alternately in any order, spooning a little tomato mixture and basil over each layer. Finish with tomato and basil, then the remaining spinach. Cover with the overhanging cling film. Chill for 4 hours, or until set.

To Serve Unfold the cling film on the top and invert the terrine onto a plate. Remove the tin and cling film. Allow to come to room temperature, about 30 minutes.

Chef's Tips

When layering the vegetables in the tin, consider colour, bearing in mind what the terrine will look like when it is sliced.

For a piquant touch, serve the terrine with curried mayonnaise: stir ¼ teaspoon ready made curry paste into 150 ml (¼ pint) mayonnaise and season with salt and a few drops of lemon juice.

You can make the terrine up to 24 hours in advance and keep it, covered with cling film, in the refrigerator.

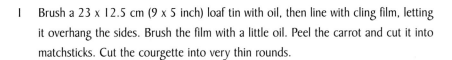

SEARED SCALLOPS WITH ROASTED PEPPER COULIS

Serves 4

Preparation time: 30 minutes

Cooking time: 2-3 minutes

Chef's Tips

Delicatessens sell roasted peppers loose by the kilo/lb and in jars. Red or yellow peppers are the best colours for making coulis. If you like, you can roast peppers yourself – see page 184.

Not all scallops come with their corals attached, but they do add a touch of colour and they taste really delicious, so try to get them if you can.

Variation

Fresh salmon or tuna can be used instead of scallops.

A FIRST COURSE WITH an elegant presentation for a special occasion. Scallops are expensive, but they are quick and easy to cook, so this is a marvellous dish you can make at short notice.

8 large scallops
juice of 2 limes
90 ml (3 fl oz) olive oil
sea salt and freshly ground black pepper
fresh coriander leaves, to garnish

Coulis

175 g (6 oz) roasted peppers
1 garlic clove, roughly chopped
100 ml (3½ fl oz) olive oil
a little lime juice

1   Separate the corals from the scallops, then cut off and discard the rubbery muscles. Slice each scallop into 2-3 discs, depending on their thickness. Place the corals and scallops in a glass or stainless steel bowl. In a separate bowl, whisk together the lime juice, all but 1 tablespoon of the olive oil and plenty of pepper, then pour over the scallops. Cover and leave to marinate for 30 minutes.

2   Meanwhile, make the coulis: drain the peppers if necessary and place them in a food processor fitted with the metal blade. Add the garlic and olive oil and work to a purée. Strain and season to taste, then add lime juice to thin the coulis down a little.

3   Drain the scallops and corals and pat them dry. Heat the remaining oil in a non-stick frying pan until hot. Add the scallops and sear quickly and lightly over high heat until nicely coloured on each side, 2-3 minutes total cooking time. Remove with a slotted spoon.

To Serve Arrange the scallops and corals on individual plates and grind a little sea salt and black pepper over them. Spoon the coulis into the middle, garnish with coriander leaves and serve.

WARM POTATO SALAD

Serves 4

Preparation time: 15 minutes

Cooking time: 20-25 minutes

Chef's Tip

For salads, waxy potatoes are best. They hold their shape better than floury potatoes. The variety called Charlotte is a good one to use. In some supermarkets, waxy varieties are described as French-style or continental potatoes.

C LASSIC FRENCH RECIPES often include a raw egg in their dressings. Here a little ready made mayonnaise is used instead to create a salad dressing which has a similar texture and flavour.

625 g (1¼ lb) new potatoes
salt and freshly ground black pepper
2 celery sticks
1 small handful of fresh coriander
150 g (5 oz) lardons or thickly diced bacon or pancetta
2–3 teaspoons Dijon mustard, to taste
4 tablespoons olive oil
juice of ½ lemon
1 tablespoon bottled mayonnaise

1 Cook the potatoes in their skins salted boiling water for 15-20 minutes until tender. Meanwhile, dice the celery and finely chop the coriander.

2 Drain the potatoes well and leave until cool enough to handle, then peel off the potato skins and thickly slice the potatoes or cut them into chunks. Put the potatoes in a warm bowl. Quickly dry-fry the lardons, bacon or pancetta in a non-stick frying pan until browned and crispy. Remove with a slotted spoon and add to the potatoes.

3 Whisk together the mustard, oil and lemon juice in a jug, pour into the frying pan and stir over high heat to deglaze. Pour immediately over the potato mixture and shake the bowl so the dressing is evenly distributed.

4 Add the celery and mayonnaise and half the coriander. Fold gently to mix. Taste and add salt and pepper, and more mustard if you like.

To Serve Turn the salad into a serving bowl and sprinkle with the remaining coriander. Serve as soon as possible, while warm.

Individual cheese soufflés

THESE ARE SIMPLE to make – it's the large soufflés that are more tricky because it is difficult to judge whether they are cooked or not – so invest in a set of ramekins and impress your friends.

40 g (1½ oz) butter, plus extra for greasing
40 g (1½ oz) plain flour, plus extra for dusting
250 ml (8 fl oz) hot milk
100 g (3½ oz) Emmenthal, Gruyère or Jarlsberg cheese, grated
3 egg yolks
¼–½ teaspoon English mustard powder, to taste
5 egg whites
pinch of salt

1   Brush six 150-200 ml (5-7 fl oz) ramekins with a little softened butter and dust with flour, shaking out any excess. Set aside in a cool place. Preheat the oven to 180°C (350°F) Gas 4.

2   Melt the butter in a medium saucepan and stir in the flour. Cook over low heat, stirring constantly, for 1 minute. Remove from the heat and whisk in the hot milk – the mixture will be very thick and stiff. Place over low heat and cook for 2-3 minutes, then stir in the grated cheese, egg yolks and mustard to taste. Keep the mixture warm.

3   In a large clean bowl, whisk the egg whites and salt until medium peaks form. Fold into the cheese sauce one-third at a time, taking care not to overmix.

4   Divide the mixture between the ramekins. Bake immediately for 10-15 minutes until well risen and golden.

To Serve   Using oven gloves, quickly transfer the ramekins to individual plates. Serve immediately.

Serves 6

Preparation time: 20 minutes

Cooking time: 10-15 minutes

Chef's Tips

Check the volume of your ramekins before starting. Some hold 250-300 ml (8-10 fl oz), in which case the amount of soufflé mixture given here will be enough for four and you will need to increase the cooking time by 3-5 minutes.

To help the soufflés rise evenly, clean the rims of the ramekins before baking by pinching the dish with your thumb on the inside and turning the dish around.

Variations

Instead of the mild cheese, you can use a mature Cheddar, or a crumbled blue cheese with 90 g (3 oz) sautéed mushrooms.

Beef carpaccio

Serves 4

Preparation time: 15 minutes,
plus 4 hours freezing

Chef's Tip

*Freezing the beef until hard is
a technique used by oriental
chefs. It is the best way to
get wafer thin slices.*

T HIS ITALIAN CLASSIC originated in the famous Harry's Bar in Venice. In Italian
restaurants it is usually served with a bottle of the best extra-virgin olive oil to
sprinkle over the beef. You can do this too if you wish.

250–300 g (8–10 oz) piece of beef fillet
salt and freshly ground black pepper
4–6 tablespoons Basil Coulis (page 185) or bottled pesto and a little olive oil
1 shallot or small onion
4 tablespoons drained capers
150 g (5 oz) block of Parmesan cheese

1 Trim any fat or sinew from the beef and discard. Wrap the beef very tightly in cling
film and place it in the freezer for about 4 hours to harden.

2 About 1 hour before serving, cut the beef into wafer thin slices, using a sawing
action with a very sharp knife. Arrange the beef on 4 plates, overlapping the slices
slightly. Season with salt and pepper and drizzle with basil coulis or with pesto
mixed to a runny consistency with olive oil. Finely chop the shallot or onion and
sprinkle over the beef with the capers.

3 Take the block of Parmesan and a vegetable peeler and carefully shave thin slivers
of cheese onto a plate. Pick up the shavings with your fingertips and place them
delicately on the carpaccio. Cover the plates and leave at room temperature for
30-45 minutes, by which time the beef will have thawed.

To Serve Uncover the plates and serve immediately, with hot crusty bread.

CRÊPES WITH WILD MUSHROOMS

Serves 4

Preparation time: 10 minutes

Cooking time:
about 15 minutes

Chef's Tip

*Ready made buckwheat
pancakes (crêpes) from
Brittany are sold in packets
in many supermarkets and
delicatessens. Apart from the
fact that they save time and
trouble, they are very good,
and lend this classic French
dish a touch of authenticity.
They are usually large, about
30 cm (12 inches) in diameter;
if you make your own crêpes,
a recipe for which is given on
page 190, they are likely to
be smaller, so you will need
2-3 crêpes per person.*

THE COMBINATION OF earthy wild mushrooms, garlic and cream makes a fabulously rich filling for crêpes. Serve before a simple main course of grilled or roast meat, poultry or fish, or as a supper dish on their own with a crisp salad to follow.

500 g (1 lb) mixed wild mushrooms
2 shallots
1 garlic clove
60 g (2 oz) butter
salt and freshly ground black pepper
100 ml (3½ fl oz) double cream
4 cooked crêpes
very finely chopped fresh flat-leaf parsley, to serve

1   Thinly slice the mushrooms. Finely chop the shallots and garlic. Melt the butter in a large frying pan and sauté the mushrooms over high heat, stirring frequently until all of their liquid has evaporated and they are tender.

2   Turn the heat down to low and add the shallots and garlic. Cook for another minute, stirring constantly, without allowing the shallots and garlic to brown. Season with salt and pepper and stir in the cream. Increase the heat to moderate and cook until very thick, about 2 minutes. Remove from the heat and keep warm.

3   Gently warm the crêpes through in a very lightly buttered non-stick frying pan over low to moderate heat. Lay the crêpes on a clean surface and spoon one-quarter of the mushroom filling in the centre of each. Fold in the sides, then make into parcels or roll up into logs.

To Serve   Place the crêpes seam-side down on individual plates and sprinkle with chopped parsley. Serve immediately.

WARM SCALLOP SALAD

A QUINTESSENTIALLY FRENCH SALAD for a special dinner party. The combination of crisp sautéed potatoes and melt-in-the-mouth scallops is absolutely delicious, and the presentation on a bed of red and green mixed leaves is really eye-catching.

8 large scallops
500 g (1 lb) peeled small potatoes
leaves of ½ head of frisée lettuce
leaves of ½ head of radicchio
4 tablespoons olive oil
salt and freshly ground black pepper
6 tablespoons Balsamic Vinaigrette (page 188)

Serves 4

Preparation time:
15-20 minutes

Cooking time:
about 15 minutes

1 Remove the corals from the scallops and cut each coral into 2-3 pieces. Cut off and discard the rubbery muscles from the scallops, then slice each scallop into 2-3 discs. Cut the potatoes into discs. Tear the salad leaves into bite-sized pieces and arrange in mounds on individual plates.

2 Heat the olive oil in a frying pan until hot. Add the potatoes, sprinkle with salt and pepper and sauté over moderate heat for about 10 minutes until nicely coloured. Transfer to kitchen paper with a slotted spoon, sprinkle with salt and drain.

3 Season the scallops. Increase the heat under the pan to high, add the scallops and corals and sauté for 3-4 minutes until seared on all sides. Remove with a slotted spoon and arrange on top of the salad leaves with the potatoes.

4 Pour the vinaigrette into the pan and stir over high heat until sizzling.

To Serve Spoon the vinaigrette over the salads and serve immediately.

Chef's Tips

Vacuum-packed peeled potatoes, called pommes parisiennes, are ideal for sautéing. Look for them in the fresh vegetable sections of supermarkets. They are completely natural, with no additives or preservatives.

Fresh scallops are best for salads. Frozen scallops tend to be watery when they are thawed.

GRILLED MUSSELS WITH LIME AND PESTO

F OR A DINNER party, these mussels can be arranged on a bed of coarse sea salt in individual gratin dishes. This way they will not only look good, but the salt will help to hold them steady.

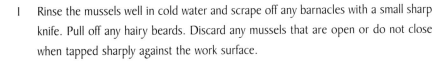

1 kg (2 lb) fresh mussels
1 shallot or small onion
250 ml (8 fl oz) dry white or red wine
1 sprig of fresh thyme
1 bay leaf
salt and freshly ground black pepper
about 4 tablespoons bottled green or red pesto
fresh basil sprigs and lime wedges, to garnish

Serves 4

Preparation time: 45 minutes

Cooking time:
about 10 minutes

1   Rinse the mussels well in cold water and scrape off any barnacles with a small sharp knife. Pull off any hairy beards. Discard any mussels that are open or do not close when tapped sharply against the work surface.

2   Finely chop the shallot or onion and place it in a saucepan with the wine, thyme, bay leaf and salt and pepper. Cover tightly and bring slowly to simmering point. Add the mussels, cover the pan again and cook, bubbling briskly, until all the shells have opened, about 3-4 minutes.

3   Drain the mussels from the cooking liquid and cool them to room temperature. Detach the top shell of each mussel, then loosen the mussels from their bottom shells but leave them in place. Spoon a little pesto over each mussel, then arrange them in individual flameproof gratin dishes.

4   Minutes before serving, preheat the grill to high. Place the mussels under the grill for about 1 minute, watching all the time, until the pesto bubbles.

To Serve   Tuck a few basil sprigs between the shells and serve immediately, with lime wedges for squeezing. French bread makes a good accompaniment.

Chef's Tip

Before buying mussels, check that they don't have too many barnacles and beards attached. Some are sold quite clean, and you will find these save you an enormous amount of preparation time.

First courses
quick and easy ideas

Nibbles and Nuts

• Dry-fry assorted nuts – cashews, peanuts, almonds, macadamias – in a small non-stick frying pan with 1 tablespoon Persian Spice Rub (page 183). Tip onto kitchen paper and leave to cool.

Ciabatta with Dips

• Serve each person with a small bowl of best-quality olive oil and chunks of fresh ciabatta for dipping.

• For a peppery bite, grind black pepper over the top.

• Add a few finely chopped black or green olives to the oil, or a spoonful of tapenade (olive and anchovy paste).

• Or add a few chopped canned anchovies or sun-dried tomatoes to the oil.

• Or whisk in a little bottled red or green pesto, sun-dried tomato paste, or Roasted Garlic flesh (page 184).

Bruschetta and Crostini

• Lightly toast thin slices of baguette, then spread with pesto or sun-dried tomato paste.

• Cover with thin slices of mozzarella or goat's cheese, then top with mixed dried herbs, canned anchovy fillets, sardines or tuna, or pan-fried thinly sliced scallops.

• Grill or bake in a hot oven for a few minutes until the cheese melts. Serve hot, garnished with sprigs of fresh herbs.

Antipasto

• Arrange a few thin slices of salami, bresàola or other cured or cooked meats on individual plates.

• Next to the meat, arrange quartered hard-boiled eggs or quails' eggs, black and green olives, bottled artichoke hearts and mushrooms, cherry tomatoes, roasted peppers, sliced mozzarella.

• You can serve just one or two of these Italian antipasto ingredients, or as many as you like.

• The aim with antipasto is to present a dish that is as colourful as it is tasty. Alternative ingredients could be chunks of tuna, strips of anchovy (draped across the hard-boiled eggs), tiny radishes, celery hearts or flageolets.

• It is customary to offer extra-virgin olive oil and wine vinegar at the table, so that your guests can dress the vegetables if they wish.

Parma Ham with Figs

- Place wafer-thin slices of Parma ham (prosciutto di Parma) on individual plates. For an attractive presentation, roll them up into cone shapes.

- Cut a cross in the tops of fresh figs, open the figs out to make flower shapes, then place next to the ham.

Smoked Salmon

- Serve thin slices of smoked salmon topped with a spoonful of soured cream and a little caviar or black lumpfish roe. Accompany with lemon or lime wedges and thinly sliced and buttered pumpernickel, rye or wholemeal bread.

- Make roulades by rolling smoked salmon slices around a filling of cream cheese, plain or mixed with finely chopped dill or snipped chives, or with chopped prawns. Garnish with dill fronds or whole chives.

- Line ramekins with thinly sliced smoked salmon, letting the slices overhang the edges. Fill with taramasalata and cover with the overhanging salmon. Turn out upside down onto individual plates and garnish with slices of black olives.

Avocado

- Cut ripe avocados in half and remove the stones. Fill the centres with flaked crabmeat mixed with mayonnaise, soured cream or fromage frais, or a mixture of these, spiked with lemon or lime juice and seasoned with salt, pepper and a drop or two of Tabasco.

- Alternate thin slices of ripe avocado, plum tomatoes and mozzarella on a platter, overlapping them slightly. Drizzle with Basil Coulis (page 185) or Balsamic Vinaigrette (page 188).

- Arrange thin slices of avocado alternately with pink grapefruit slices and drizzle with Vinaigrette (page 188).

Melon

- Cut baby melons (charentais, cantaloupe or ogen) in half and scoop out the seeds. Cut a very thin slice from the base of each, then stand the melon halves upright on individual plates. Pour port or Madeira into the centre.

- Cut chilled ripe cantaloupe or ogen melon into thin slices, removing the seeds and skin. Arrange the slices in a fan shape and sprinkle with a little lemon juice. Serve with wafer-thin slices of Parma ham, sprinkled with freshly ground black pepper.

Prawns

- Serve cooked tiger or king prawns in their shells with Aïoli (garlic mayonnaise, page 189) for dipping. Provide finger bowls and napkins.

- Toss peeled cooked prawns with crème fraîche or mayonnaise (or both), lime juice, grated fresh root ginger and chopped fresh coriander. Season with a dash of fish sauce and serve in Little Gem lettuce cups. Add a little chopped fresh chilli if you like a hot flavour.

Soup

- Dress up canned tomato soup or consommé by adding a spoonful or two of sherry, vermouth, port or Madeira.

- Whisk a little dry white wine and cream or crème fraîche into a canned smooth soup such as chicken, mushroom or tomato, and serve swirled with cream, feathering it with the handle of a teaspoon.

- Whisk a spoonful or two of bottled pesto or Roasted Garlic flesh (page 184) into vegetable soups.

- Just before serving, sprinkle soup with chopped or shredded fresh herbs, or a single sprig or leaf.

- A liberal sprinkling of black pepper can also be used as a garnish, or a little freshly grated nutmeg, finely grated or shredded cheese, or Parmesan curls.

After Work

2

T HE MOST DEMANDING meals to cook are the everyday ones – the suppers you put together after a busy day at work, when so often you are both tired and rushed.

The recipes in this chapter have been chosen with this in mind, combining a few freshly bought ingredients with storecupboard basics, and preparing and cooking them as quickly as possible. There are recipes for eggs, pasta, rice, fish, poultry, meat and vegetables, giving you lots of choice. There are also plenty of ideas for variations and alternative ingredients, so you can use what you have to hand rather than having to make a special shopping trip to buy something new.

The key to creating imaginative and easy weekday meals is a well-stocked storecupboard, and if you turn to page 182 you will find a list of all the essential items for the recipes in this book. Here you will see a variety of ingredients from around the world, because today's Le Cordon Bleu recipes combine the traditional and the modern with a fusion of flavours from both east and west. In this exciting collection you will find French fused with Thai, Italian, Spanish, Indian, Scandinavian, Chinese, American and many other influences, all featured in recipes based on professional yet simple cooking techniques. They will add excitement and sophistication to your cooking, whether you want a warming winter soup, a light summer salad or a special main course to entertain friends in the middle of the working week.

The recipes in this chapter have been created to make light work of everyday cooking, and to make every after-work supper exactly what it should be – the most relaxing meal of the day.

FRENCH ONION SOUP

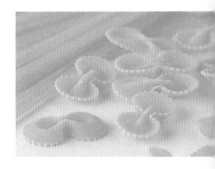

THIS IS THE perfect winter warmer. Everyone loves it, and it tastes best if made the day before, so it's the perfect thing for an informal midweek supper with friends or family.

2 large Spanish onions, total weight about 500 g (1 lb)
2 x 295 g cans condensed beef consommé
90 g (3 oz) butter
salt and freshly ground black pepper
4 teaspoons plain flour
125 ml (4 fl oz) dry white wine
1 bouquet garni
6–9 slices of baguette
60–90 g (2–3 oz) Emmenthal, Gruyère or Jarlsberg cheese
2–3 tablespoons port or Madeira (optional)

Serves 2-3

Preparation time:
15-20 minutes

Cooking time: about 1 hour

1   Halve the onions lengthways and finely slice them. Make the consommé up to 1.2 litres (2 pints) with water and heat to boiling. Keep hot.

2   Melt the butter in a large saucepan over low heat. Add the onions, stir well and season with a generous pinch of salt. Cover and cook gently for 5 minutes. Remove the lid, increase the heat to moderate and cook the onions until a light golden brown in colour, 12-15 minutes. Stir frequently during this time and watch carefully towards the end of cooking to prevent the onions catching on the bottom of the pan.

3   Stir in the flour and cook for 1-2 minutes, then add the wine and bring to the boil. Cook for 1 minute, stirring constantly to loosen the browned pieces of onion on the bottom of the pan. Add the hot consommé and the bouquet garni, stir well and bring to the boil. Cover and simmer gently for 30 minutes.

4   Meanwhile, preheat the grill and lightly toast the slices of baguette on both sides. Leave the grill on. Thinly slice the cheese and arrange it on top of the baguette. Remove the bouquet garni from the soup, stir in the port or Madeira (if using), then season the soup to taste.

To Serve   Ladle the soup into individual flameproof bowls. Top each serving with 3 slices of baguette and put under the grill until the cheese melts and bubbles. Serve.

Chef's Tips

Don't skimp on the browning time for the onions – this is essential to give the soup a good colour and flavour.

If you don't have port or Madeira, you can use sherry or brandy, or leave it out altogether.

If making the day before, cook the soup up to the end of step 3, then remove the bouquet garni. Cool, cover and refrigerate the soup. Before serving, reheat the soup until bubbling, preheat the grill and prepare the croûtes.

LENTIL SOUP

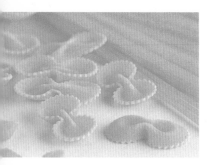

THIS IS A thick, textured soup, ideal for a hearty supper with crusty French bread and cheese. For a dinner party first course, it can be made to look elegant by being puréed, then sieved and served garnished with small celery leaves.

1 small onion
1 small carrot
1 small celery stick
1 garlic clove
90 g (3 oz) smoked bacon rashers
125 g (4 oz) French green lentils
1.5 litres (2½ pints) hot chicken or vegetable stock
1 bouquet garni
salt and freshly ground black pepper

Serves 2-3

Preparation time: 10 minutes

Cooking time: 1 hour

1   Finely chop the onion, carrot, celery and garlic. Cut the bacon into small pieces with scissors, discarding any rind.

2   Put the lentils in a large saucepan, cover with cold water and bring to the boil. Drain into a sieve, rinse under the cold tap, then return to the pan.

3   Add the stock to the lentils with the chopped vegetables, bacon and bouquet garni. Bring to the boil, then half cover and simmer over moderate heat until the lentils are very soft, about 1 hour. Stir occasionally during cooking and add a little water if the consistency of the soup is too thick.

To Serve   Remove the bouquet garni, then season the soup to taste. Serve hot.

Chef's Tips

French green lentils are sold in supermarkets, delicatessens and health food shops. The best are Le Puy lentils, which have a nutty flavour and retain their shape well during cooking. Although French chefs always use them, they are not essential for this soup – you could use red or orange lentils instead.

You can cut down preparation time by chopping all the vegetables in a food processor fitted with the metal blade.

CORN AND POTATO CHOWDER

A FAVOURITE AMERICAN SOUP that makes a warming and filling meal in winter. Serve with crusty baguette and follow with a green salad, or maybe some cheese and fresh fruit, such as apples and grapes.

1 small onion
2 garlic cloves
375 g (12 oz) potatoes
2 tablespoons olive oil
800 ml (1⅓ pints) hot chicken or vegetable stock
salt and freshly ground black pepper
1 x 198 g can sweetcorn with sweet peppers, drained
150 ml (¼ pint) double cream
chopped fresh parsley or coriander, to garnish

Serves 2-3

Preparation time: 10 minutes

Cooking time:
about 40 minutes

1   Finely chop the onion and garlic, keeping them separate. Peel the potatoes and cut them into small cubes. Heat the oil in a saucepan and cook the onion over low heat for 2-3 minutes until softened. Add the garlic and potatoes and cook, stirring, for a few minutes.

2   Add the hot stock, season and bring to the boil over high heat. Cover and simmer over low to moderate heat until the potatoes are very soft, about 30 minutes. Add the sweetcorn and peppers and the cream. Heat through, stirring, until bubbling.

To Serve   Taste for seasoning and sprinkle with chopped parsley or coriander.

Variations

There are many ways in which you can vary chowder. Some cooks like to use milk instead of stock, or half stock and half milk. Chopped bacon is often fried with the onion at the beginning, or cubed ham added at the end. Smoked fish chowder is a classic – cut 250 g (8 oz) smoked cod or haddock into large chunks and add them for the last 5 minutes. Flaked canned tuna is another popular fish to use: simply stir it in with the sweetcorn.

PASTA ALLA DIAVOLA

ALLA DIAVOLA MEANS 'DEVILLED', a name sometimes used to describe dishes containing chillies. Often such dishes come from southern Italy and Sicily, a legacy from the days when the Arabs settled there.

250 g (8 oz) spaghetti or other pasta of your choice
salt and freshly ground black pepper
flesh from a few cloves of Roasted Garlic (page 184)
8 tablespoons olive oil
¼–½ teaspoon crushed dried chillies, or to taste
freshly grated Parmesan cheese, to serve

Serves 2

Preparation time: 5 minutes, plus time to make the roasted garlic

Cooking time: 10-12 minutes

Chef's Tip

This simple pasta dish should be made with a good quality, cold-pressed virgin olive oil. There are very few other ingredients, so the fruity flavour of the oil can be fully appreciated.

1   Cook the pasta in salted boiling water according to packet instructions.

2   Meanwhile, put the roasted garlic flesh in a bowl with the olive oil and mash with a fork.

3   Drain the pasta. Heat the garlic oil in the pan in which the pasta was cooked. Add the pasta and chillies and quickly toss together. Taste for seasoning.

To Serve   Divide the pasta equally between 2 warm bowls and serve immediately, topped with Parmesan.

Pasta with Italian sausage and aubergines

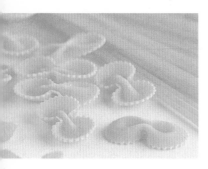

THIS HEARTY PASTA dish comes from northern Italy, where robustly flavoured meat sauces are very popular. If you are a vegetarian, just omit the sausages – the sauce tastes good with or without them.

1 small onion
2 garlic cloves
1 aubergine, weighing about 150 g (5 oz)
3 tablespoons olive oil
about 175 g (6 oz) Italian sausages
salt and freshly ground black pepper
1 x 400 g can chopped tomatoes
1 tablespoon tomato purée
250–375 g (8–12 oz) pasta
freshly grated Parmesan cheese, to serve

Serves 3-4

Preparation time: 10 minutes

Cooking time:
about 30 minutes

Chef's Tip

Italian sausages can be found in some large supermarkets, but for the best choice go to an Italian delicatessen and ask for salsiccia puro suino – fresh pure pork sausage. It comes in many different shapes and sizes, and can be mild or spicy. Luganega is a popular variety that is easy to find. You can of course use other sausages if you prefer.

1 Finely chop the onion and garlic, keeping them separate. Halve and dice the aubergine. Heat 1 tablespoon of the oil in a sauté pan and brown the sausages in it. Remove them with a slotted spoon and set aside on kitchen paper.

2 Heat the remaining oil in the pan, add the onion and cook over low heat until softened, then add the aubergine and garlic with a good pinch of salt. Stir over moderate heat until the aubergine begins to soften and colour.

3 Add the tomatoes, tomato purée and 175 ml (6 fl oz) water. Bring to a simmer and cook for 10 minutes, stirring occasionally. Meanwhile, cook the pasta in salted boiling water according to packet instructions.

4 Cut the sausages into thick slices and add to the sauce. Cook for 5-10 minutes more, then season to taste.

To Serve Drain the pasta and turn it into a warm bowl. Pour the sauce over the pasta and toss to mix. Serve immediately, with Parmesan cheese.

PASTA ALLE VONGOLE

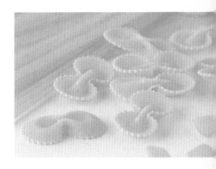

MANY TRADITIONAL ITALIAN recipes use fresh clams. For speed and convenience, bottled clams are used here – a handy storecupboard item that Italian cooks tend to rely on a lot.

250 g (8 oz) pasta
salt and freshly ground black pepper
2–3 garlic cloves
1 x 200 g can or jar clams in brine
6 tablespoons olive oil
3–4 tablespoons finely chopped fresh flat-leaf parsley, to serve

1 Cook the pasta in salted boiling water according to packet instructions.

2 Meanwhile, finely chop the garlic and drain and roughly chop the clams. Heat the oil in a saucepan, add the garlic and cook over very low heat for 1-2 minutes. Stir constantly and watch carefully so that the garlic does not brown.

3 Add the chopped clams, stir and season well.

To Serve Drain the pasta and return it to the pan. Add the clam sauce and chopped parsley and toss to mix. Serve immediately, in warm bowls.

Serves 2

Preparation time: 5 minutes

Cooking time:
10-12 minutes

Chef's Tips

In Italy, clam sauce is usually served with a long thin pasta such as linguine, spaghetti or spaghettini, but you can use any pasta shape you like.

Take care not to boil the clams or they may become rubbery. They are already cooked, and only need heating through.

Variations

If you like tomato sauce with clams, add 1 x 400 g can chopped tomatoes after softening the garlic and cook for about 10 minutes. A splash of dry white wine can also be added, whether you use tomatoes or not.

RISOTTO WITH PEAS AND PROSCIUTTO

A RISOTTO IS THE ideal dish for a midweek evening meal because it is so quick to prepare and cook. If you have friends round, serve it with crusty ciabatta, some Italian cheese and a tossed green salad – and a bottle of Italian wine of course.

1 small onion
125 g (4 oz) prosciutto (Parma ham)
800–900 ml (1⅓–1½ pints) hot chicken or vegetable stock
1 fresh thyme sprig
1 bay leaf
90 g (3 oz) butter
200 g (7 oz) short grain risotto rice (arborio or carnaroli)
125 ml (4 fl oz) dry white wine
125 g (4 oz) frozen peas
salt and freshly ground black pepper
fresh Parmesan cheese shavings, to serve

Serves 2-3

Preparation time: 10 minutes

Cooking time:
20-25 minutes

1   Finely chop the onion. Cut the prosciutto into thin strips. Bring the stock to the boil in a saucepan with the thyme and bay leaf and keep at simmering point.

2   Melt the butter in a heavy flameproof casserole, add the onion and cook over moderate heat until soft. Add the rice and stir for 1-2 minutes until the grains are coated in butter.

3   Add the wine. Stir until the liquid has been absorbed completely, then begin adding the simmering stock a ladleful at a time, allowing the rice to absorb the stock before adding more. Once half the stock has been absorbed, add the frozen peas, then continue cooking and adding more stock until the rice is al dente. The consistency should be moist and creamy, but not too runny.

To Serve Stir in the prosciutto and seasoning to taste. Remove from the heat and allow to rest for about 2 minutes. Serve topped with Parmesan cheese shavings.

Variation

Substitute 2 Italian sausages for the prosciutto and 1 red and 1 green pepper for the peas. Remove the casings from the sausages and dice the peppers. Fry the meat from the sausages with the onion until browned, add the peppers and continue as described in the recipe. Stir in 2 tablespoons shredded fresh basil just before serving.

SCRAMBLED EGGS WITH SMOKED SALMON

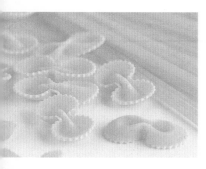

Serves 2

Preparation time: 5 minutes

Cooking time: 5-8 minutes

Chef's Tips

Look for packets of smoked salmon trimmings in your supermarket. They are less expensive than whole slices.

To accompany the scrambled eggs, sauté 200 g (7 oz) chanterelle mushrooms and 1 tablespoon finely chopped shallot in 60 g (2 oz) butter. Mix in 1 tablespoon finely chopped fresh parsley.

Variation

For a luxurious brunch dish, replace the smoked salmon with 60 g (2 oz) caviar. Don't stir it into the eggs, simply spoon it on top of the eggs just before serving and garnish with a sprig of chervil. For a less expensive dish that looks equally impressive use lumpfish roe instead of caviar.

F OR A QUICK and nutritious after-work supper, nothing beats scrambled eggs on toast. Here they are given a luxurious touch with smoked salmon and cream. Serve them moist and creamy, to contrast with the crispness of the toast.

125 g (4 oz) smoked salmon
1 small handful of fresh chives
6 large eggs
salt and freshly ground black pepper
2 tablespoons double cream
30 g (1 oz) butter

1   Cut the smoked salmon into thin strips. Snip the chives finely with scissors, reserving a few whole stems for the garnish. Break the eggs into a bowl, season, then add the cream. Whisk lightly, just enough to break up the yolks a little.

2   Heat the butter until foaming in a medium non-stick sauté pan or a wide shallow saucepan. Add the eggs and cook over low heat, stirring constantly and slowly with a wooden spatula until the eggs are only just beginning to set. They should still be creamy and moist.

3   Remove from the heat and gently stir in the smoked salmon. Taste for seasoning.

To Serve   Spoon onto buttered toasted rye bread, muffins or bagels, garnish with the reserved chives and serve immediately.

Omelette Arnold Bennett

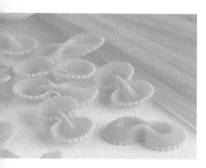

Serves 2

Preparation time:
10-15 minutes

Cooking time:
about 10 minutes

Chef's Tip

One of the secrets of a good omelette is the pan in which you cook it. French chefs keep a well-seasoned cast iron pan especially for omelettes, never using it for anything else. It is not washed after use, but simply wiped with kitchen paper. A good quality, heavy non-stick pan is also good for omelettes, and 15–18 cm (6–7 inches) is the perfect size for a 2-egg omelette to serve 2 people. This is by far the easiest size to make, so if you are serving 4, it is better to make 2 separate omelettes than 1 large one.

THIS CLASSIC RECIPE was created for the writer by the chefs at the Savoy in London. It is still on the menu there. In the Savoy recipe the eggs are separated, the whites lightly beaten and folded into the yolks. This version is quicker and simpler.

175–200 g (6–7 oz) smoked haddock fillet
about 400 ml (14 fl oz) milk and water, mixed half and half
100 ml (3½ fl oz) double cream
2 large eggs
pinch of cayenne pepper
freshly ground black pepper
2 teaspoons sunflower oil
30–60 g (1–2 oz) Parmesan cheese
snipped fresh chives, to garnish

1   Put the smoked haddock in a small pan and add enough milk and water to cover the fish. Heat to simmering point, then half cover and poach over low heat for 5 minutes.

2   Remove the fish with a slotted spoon and drain, then break it into its natural flakes, removing any skin and bones. Drain the fish again, place in a bowl and fold in half the cream. Beat the remaining cream with the eggs, cayenne and black pepper. Preheat the grill.

3   Heat the oil in an omelette pan or frying pan which can safely be used under the grill. When very hot, pour in the egg mixture. Stir with a wooden spatula until setting around the edges, then spoon the haddock and cream over the middle. Cook for a further 2-3 minutes or until the omelette has set underneath.

4   Grate the Parmesan over the omelette, then flash under the grill for 1-2 minutes until golden brown.

To Serve Slide the omelette out of the pan onto a plate and sprinkle with chives. Serve hot, cut into wedges.

EGG PANCAKES WITH SALMON AND HERBS

A FUSION OF ORIENTAL-STYLE pancakes and Scandinavian filling makes a very tasty supper dish for 2 people. Serve with a leafy green or mixed salad tossed in Vinaigrette (page 188).

4 large eggs
about 2 teaspoons sunflower oil

Filling

1 shallot or 2 spring onions
2 tablespoons sunflower oil
1 tablespoon sesame oil
300 g (10 oz) salmon fillet
¼ teaspoon each ground cumin and coriander
1–2 tablespoons chopped fresh dill
salt and freshly ground black pepper
fresh dill sprigs, to garnish

Serves 2

Preparation time: 20 minutes

Cooking time:
about 20 minutes

1   First make the filling. Finely chop the shallot or spring onions. Heat the oils in a frying pan until hot, add the salmon and fry over moderate heat for 3 minutes on each side. Remove the pan from the heat and lift the salmon out with a fish slice. Flake the salmon, discarding any skin and bones.

2   Return the pan to the heat, add the shallot or spring onions and the spices and stir for 1 minute. Add the salmon, dill and seasoning and toss to combine. Remove from the heat and keep hot while making the pancakes.

3   Beat the eggs with 100 ml (3½ fl oz) water, a little salt and plenty of pepper. Lightly oil a 15-18 cm (6-7 inch) omelette or frying pan and heat until very hot. Pour in one-quarter of the egg mixture and cook like an omelette until set on top and golden underneath, 2-3 minutes. Slide out of the pan onto a plate and keep hot. Repeat with the remaining egg mixture to make 4 pancakes altogether, stacking them on top of each other.

To Serve Spoon one-quarter of the filling in the centre of each pancake, fold one side over the filling to cover it, then bring the other side over to overlap slightly. Arrange a sprig of dill in the centre of each pancake and serve immediately.

Chef's Tips

These pancakes are extra good if you put a spoonful of crème fraîche on top of the filling before folding, or if you serve them with a separate bowl of crème fraîche mixed with chopped fresh dill and salt and pepper.

They also make a very good first course for 4 people. Use 2 large eggs and 4 table-spoons water to make 4 very thin pancakes and top the filling with crème fraîche before folding.

ROCKET WITH SAUTÉED POTATOES AND BACON

This is a good way to use up leftover boiled or baked potatoes, but if you don't have any, you can buy vacuum packs of peeled potatoes for convenience. They cook very quickly, and have no additives, preservatives or colourings.

175–250 g (6–8 oz) diced bacon
500 g (1 lb) cold cooked potatoes
1–2 tablespoons olive oil
125 g (4 oz) rocket
125 g (4 oz) oak leaf lettuce, lollo rosso or other salad leaves of your choice
1 quantity Mustard Vinaigrette (page 188)
salt and freshly ground black pepper

Serves 2

Preparation time:
10-15 minutes

Cooking time:
about 15 minutes

1   Put the diced bacon in a non-stick frying pan and cook, stirring frequently, over moderate heat for 5-8 minutes until browned and quite crisp. Meanwhile, slice or dice the cold potatoes.

2   Remove the bacon from the pan with a slotted spoon. Add olive oil to the pan (the amount needed will depend on how fatty the bacon was) and heat until hot. Add the potatoes and sauté for 8-10 minutes until nicely coloured and crisp. Return the bacon to the pan and toss with the potatoes.

3   Put the rocket and other salad leaves in a bowl with the potatoes and bacon. Pour in the vinaigrette, add seasoning to taste and toss to mix.

To Serve   Divide the salad equally between 2 plates and serve immediately.

Chef's Tip

Diced streaky bacon can be found in packets in most supermarkets. It saves preparation time and is well worth buying. If you see diced pancetta, an Italian dry-cured ham, this is worth trying as an alternative. It tastes a little stronger and saltier than bacon.

THAI VEGETABLE STIR-FRY

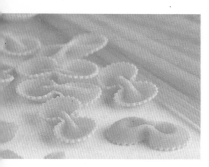

FRESH AND COLOURFUL, this tasty stir-fry makes a good vegetarian supper when served with boiled rice or noodles. The ginger gives the dish a wonderful flavour, and the aroma is quite tantalizing.

1 onion
1 fresh red or green chilli
2 garlic cloves
175–200 g (6–7 oz) broccoli florets
1 red pepper
5 cm (2 inch) piece of fresh root ginger
250 g (8 oz) fresh shiitake or oyster mushrooms
1 x 150 g can baby corn in brine
3 tablespoons sunflower oil
a good pinch of sugar, or more to taste
2–3 tablespoons fish sauce, or to taste
2–3 tablespoons soy sauce, or to taste
250 g (8 oz) bean sprouts

Serves 2

Preparation time: 15 minutes

Cooking time:
about 10 minutes

Chef's Tips

If you keep fresh root ginger in the freezer you will find it very easy to peel and grate.

For a very hot stir-fry, leave the seeds in the chilli when slicing it. For a milder flavour scrape the seeds out and discard them.

If you can't find canned baby corn, use fresh corn and boil it for 8 minutes before adding it to the stir-fry.

1   Thinly slice the onion. Thinly slice the chilli at an angle. Crush the garlic. Divide the broccoli into tiny sprigs and trim the stalks. Cut the red pepper into thin strips. Peel and grate the ginger. Thinly slice the mushrooms. Drain the corn.

2   Heat the oil in a wok or deep sauté pan, add the onion and stir-fry over low to moderate heat for a few minutes until lightly coloured. Sprinkle in the chilli, garlic and sugar, then add the broccoli and increase the heat to moderately high. Stir-fry for 3 minutes.

3   Add the red pepper, ginger and mushrooms and stir-fry for about 3 minutes, then add the fish sauce and soy sauce and stir well. Add the corn and bean sprouts and toss over high heat until all the vegetables have heated through and are well mixed.

To Serve Taste and add more sugar, fish sauce or soy sauce. Serve immediately, with extra fish sauce or soy sauce at the table.

SPINACH SALAD WITH LARDONS, CROÛTONS AND CHEESE

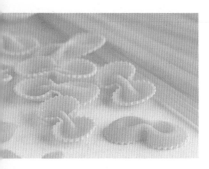

A NUTRITIOUS MAIN COURSE salad for when you crave something crisp and fresh for supper. It is based on fresh ingredients that you can pick up at the supermarket on your way home from work.

150–175 g (5–6 oz) small tender spinach leaves
90 g (3 oz) Cheddar cheese
1 tablespoon sunflower oil
200 g (7 oz) lardons
90 g (3 oz) croûtons

Dressing

2 tablespoons red wine vinegar
salt and freshly ground black pepper
90 ml (3 fl oz) sunflower oil

Serves 2-3

Preparation time: 10 minutes

Cooking time: 7-8 minutes

Chef's Tips

This salad can be made very quickly if you buy a bag of ready trimmed and washed baby spinach leaves from the supermarket, plus ready made croûtons and lardons.

If you can't find croûtons, make them yourself from day-old bread. Remove the crusts from 3 slices of sandwich bread, cut the bread into small cubes and shallow-fry in 2 tablespoons very hot oil for about 5 minutes. Drain well on kitchen paper.

Lardons are sold in packets in many supermarkets. If you can't find them, buy bacon chops and dice them. Bacon rashers are a little too thin to make good lardons.

1   Wash the spinach and remove the stalks. Drain and spin-dry the spinach leaves, then place them in a large bowl. Shred or dice the cheese, add to the bowl and toss to mix.

2   Heat the oil in a non-stick frying pan, add the lardons, bacon or pancetta and fry over moderate to high heat for about 5 minutes until crisp. Toss the lardons and shake the pan constantly. Remove with a slotted spoon and drain on kitchen paper.

3   Make the dressing. Pour the vinegar into the pan, add salt and pepper and stir over moderate heat until the salt has dissolved. Remove from the heat and slowly whisk in the remaining oil.

To Serve Pour the dressing over the salad and toss to mix. Sprinkle the bacon and croûtons on top and serve immediately.

FRITTATA

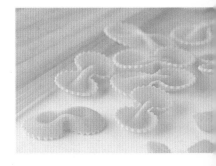

THIS FLAT ITALIAN omelette makes a nutritious and satisfying meal served with new potatoes and a crisp salad. It is just as good cold as hot, so any leftovers can be eaten as a snack or lunch next day.

100 g (3½ oz) broccoli florets
salt and freshly ground black pepper
100 g (3½ oz) button mushrooms
3 spring onions
1 garlic clove
90 g (3 oz) mature Cheddar cheese
8 large eggs
3 tablespoons olive oil

Serves 2-3

Preparation time: 10 minutes

Cooking time:
about 15 minutes

1   Divide the broccoli into tiny sprigs and trim the stalks, then drop into salted boiling water and bring back to the boil. Drain, refresh immediately in cold water, then drain and leave to dry on kitchen paper. Thinly slice the mushrooms and spring onions and finely chop the garlic. Grate the cheese. Whisk the eggs in a bowl with salt and pepper.

2   Preheat the oven to 200°C (400°F) Gas 6. Heat the oil in a large frying pan (see Chef's Tips) and sauté the mushrooms until lightly coloured. Add the spring onions and garlic. Sauté for 2 minutes, then add the broccoli and stir well to mix. Pour half the eggs over the vegetables and sprinkle with half the cheese. Cook for about 5 minutes until lightly set, then pour in the remaining eggs and sprinkle with the remaining cheese.

3   Cook in the oven for 5 minutes or until the frittata is firm and golden brown.

To Serve   Either slice the frittata in the pan and serve on individual plates, or slide out of the pan onto a platter and cut into slices. Serve hot or cold.

Chef's Tips

Make sure the pan handle is ovenproof or removeable; if not, wrap it in a double thickness of foil. If you find it more convenient, you can simply slide the pan under a hot grill to finish cooking.

Cut into thick wedges, cold frittata makes excellent picnic food. It is also good cut into small diamonds or squares to serve as a canapé with drinks.

Variations

This is a good way to use up any leftover vegetables such as peppers (roasted or plain), beans, peas, cauliflower, etc. Slices of cooked chicken, ham, spicy sausage or salami can also be added.

FISH WITH TOMATOES AND OLIVES

Serves 4

Preparation time: 10 minutes

Cooking time: 35 minutes

Chef's Tip

Thick cod fillets are very white and meaty, but delicate in texture, so take care not to let them break up during cooking. If you leave the skin on, this will help keep the fillets intact, but you may prefer to remove it – most people prefer fish served without skin.

Variations

Tuna or swordfish steaks or monkfish fillet can be used instead of cod.

To save time, you can use chopped tomatoes or bottled passata (sieved tomatoes), some brands of which have onion, garlic and herbs added. In this case, simply simmer for 10-15 minutes before adding the fish.

EADY WITH THE Provençal aromas and flavours of tomatoes, garlic and thyme, this makes an excellent main course for midweek entertaining. Serve it with couscous, rice, Mashed Potatoes (page 135) or pasta and follow with a tossed green salad.

1 x 700–800 g can whole peeled tomatoes
1 small onion
4 garlic cloves
60 g (2 oz) stoned green or black olives
125 ml (4 fl oz) olive oil
1 bay leaf
2 fresh thyme sprigs
salt and freshly ground black pepper
4 thick cod fillets, each weighing about 175 g (6 oz)
fresh thyme sprigs, to garnish (optional)

1   Tip the tomatoes into a sieve placed over a bowl and let the juice run through. Turn the tomatoes into a food processor and, using the pulse button, chop them lightly. Finely chop the onion and garlic. Quarter the olives lengthways.

2   Heat two-thirds of the oil in a large, deep sauté pan over low heat. Add the onion and cook for 2-3 minutes without colouring, then add the tomato liquid, garlic, bay leaf and thyme. Increase the heat to moderate and cook, stirring occasionally, until reduced by half. Add the tomatoes and simmer over low heat, stirring occasionally, for 30 minutes or until the sauce is thick.

3   About 10 minutes before the sauce is ready, cook the fish. Season the fish fillets and heat the remaining oil in another large, deep sauté pan. Pan-fry the fish over moderate heat for 6 minutes, turning once.

4   Remove the bay leaf and thyme from the sauce, then pour the sauce over the fish and sprinkle in the olives and seasoning to taste. Shake the pan to coat the fish in the sauce.

To Serve   Place the fish fillets on warm plates with the sauce spooned over and around. Garnish with thyme (if using) and serve immediately.

SALMON FILLETS WITH SESAME CRUST

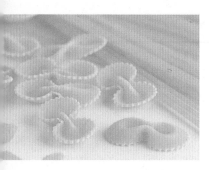

THIS IS AN excellent main course if you are entertaining a friend after work, and it is easy to increase the quantities if there are more than two of you. Broccoli or mangetouts would make a good accompaniment, or a mixed vegetable stir-fry.

4 tablespoons sesame seeds
2 thick salmon fillets, each weighing 150–175 g (5–6 oz), skinned
salt and freshly ground black pepper
2–3 tablespoons oyster sauce
1 tablespoon sunflower oil
1 tablespoon sesame oil

Serves 2

Preparation time: 5 minutes

**Cooking time:
about 10 minutes**

To Serve

2 lime wedges
oyster sauce

Chef's Tip

Salmon fillets are sold in packets in the fresh fish sections of supermarkets. Look for fillets that are about 2.5 cm (1 inch) thick. They should be boneless, but always check for any fine pin bones before cooking, and pull them out with tweezers or your fingertips. Rinse the fish before using and pat dry with kitchen paper.

1   Dry-fry the sesame seeds in a non-stick frying pan over moderate heat for 2-3 minutes until lightly toasted. Preheat the grill.

2   Cut each salmon fillet in half, then season with salt and pepper. Brush generously with oyster sauce and coat with the toasted sesame seeds.

3   Heat the oils in a non-stick frying pan until hot. Place the salmon in the pan and cook over moderate to high heat until the edges have become firm, about 3 minutes. Cook the salmon on one side only – do not turn it over.

4   Using a fish slice and keeping the fish the same way up, transfer the salmon to the grill pan. Finish cooking under the grill for about 3 minutes.

To Serve Arrange the salmon fillets on warm plates with lime wedges for squeezing. Serve extra oyster sauce in a small bowl alongside.

THAI FISH CAKES

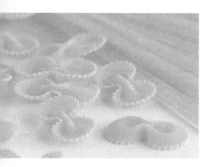

Serves 4

Preparation time: 10 minutes

Cooking time: 5-10 minutes

Chef's Tips

If you prepare the mixture the day before, turn it into a bowl, cover and refrigerate. Use within 24 hours.

Don't overwork the mixture in the food processor because this will toughen the fish, and only fry the fish cakes for the time given in the recipe. Overcooked fish cakes tend to be rubbery.

Variations

For a first course, make the fish cakes half the size. For pre-dinner nibbles or canapés, make them bite-sized and serve them on cocktail sticks. They can even be served cold, and taste good with a dip made of mayonnaise flavoured with Thai curry paste.

IF YOU HAVE a food processor, nothing could be quicker and easier than these spicy hot fish cakes, and they can be prepared up to the frying stage the day before. Serve them with a mixed salad or stir-fried vegetables.

500 g (1 lb) cod fillets, skinned
1 medium red pepper
1 large egg
2 tablespoons fish sauce
1 tablespoon red or green Thai curry paste
finely grated rind of 1 lime
1 large handful of fresh coriander leaves
good pinch of salt
4–6 tablespoons sunflower oil

To Serve

lime wedges
fish sauce (optional)

1   Cut the fish into chunks, checking carefully that there are no bones. Roughly chop the red pepper, removing the core, seeds and spongy ribs. Put the fish and red pepper in the bowl of a food processor and add the egg, fish sauce, curry paste, lime rind, coriander leaves and salt. Work to a coarse purée.

2   Heat about 2.5 cm (1 inch) oil in a frying pan until very hot. Remove the blade from the food processor bowl, then scoop out the fish mixture in heaped spoonfuls, about the size of the palm of your hand. Drop the mixture into the hot oil and flatten slightly with the back of the spoon.

3   Cook the fish cakes over moderate to high heat for 2-3 minutes on each side until golden brown. The mixture makes about 16 fish cakes, so you will need to cook them in 2-3 batches to avoid overcrowding the pan. Remove them with a slotted spoon, drain on kitchen paper and keep hot.

To Serve Arrange on a warm platter with lime wedges and serve hot. Fish sauce can be served in a small bowl, to be sprinkled over the fish cakes or used as a dip.

SALMON WITH ROSEMARY CREAM

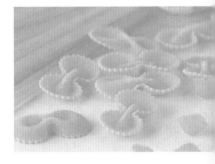

A FABULOUS MAIN COURSE for a midweek supper party. The rosemary cream sauce tastes divine, and it can be made the day before, so all you have to do on the night is quickly pan-fry the fish. Serve with baby new potatoes and mangetouts.

500 ml (16 fl oz) fish stock
1 fresh rosemary sprig
200 ml (7 fl oz) double cream
90 g (3 oz) butter
salt and white pepper
1 tablespoon sunflower oil
4 thick salmon fillets, each weighing 150–175 g (5–6 oz)
4 fresh rosemary sprigs, to garnish

1 Put the fish stock and rosemary in a saucepan and bring to the boil, then simmer gently until the stock has reduced to about half its original volume. Add the cream and continue simmering until reduced by about half again. Strain and discard the rosemary. Whisk 60 g (2 oz) of the butter into the reduced stock and cream mixture and season to taste. Set aside.

2 Check the salmon and remove any pin bones. Rinse the fish and pat dry. Melt the remaining butter with the oil in a frying pan over moderate heat. Season the salmon, place the fillets flesh side down in the pan and cook for 2-3 minutes, depending on the thickness of the fish. Carefully turn the salmon over and cook the skin side for 2-3 minutes. Remove and blot on kitchen paper.

To Serve Gently reheat the sauce, then spoon in a pool on 4 warm plates. Place a salmon fillet on top, drizzle with a little more sauce and garnish with a sprig of rosemary. Serve immediately.

Serves 4

Preparation time:
2-3 minutes

Cooking time:
about 20 minutes

Chef's Tips

Look for cans of fish stock in your supermarket – it has a much better flavour than fish stock cubes. A 425 g can will yield the right volume for this recipe.

If you can't get fresh rosemary sprigs, use about 1 tablespoon dried rosemary and tie it in a small piece of muslin.

PRAWNS WITH ORANGE AND GINGER

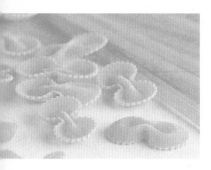

A SPEEDY STIR-FRY that takes next to no time to prepare and cook. You can make it as hot and spicy as you like – the sweet tang of the fresh oranges provides a refreshing contrast to the heat of the chillies. Serve with noodles or rice for a complete meal.

5 cm (2 inch) piece of fresh root ginger

2 garlic cloves

1 tablespoon sesame oil

¼–½ teaspoon crushed dried chillies, or to taste

salt and freshly ground black pepper

500 g (1 lb) peeled raw tiger king prawns, thawed if frozen

1 large red pepper

6 spring onions

2 large oranges

1 tablespoon sunflower oil

Serves 3-4

Preparation time: 5 minutes, plus 10-15 minutes marinating

Cooking time: 8 minutes

Chef's Tip.

Fully peeled raw tiger king prawns are sold both frozen and chilled in supermarkets. If they are frozen, they should be thawed for a maximum of 2-3 hours before cooking. If you don't have this amount of time, put them in a sieve and hold them under the cold tap, separating them with your fingers until they soften. Dry them well on kitchen paper.

1 Peel the ginger and grate it into a bowl. Finely chop the garlic and add to the ginger with the sesame oil, crushed chillies and black pepper to taste. Add the prawns and toss until coated. Cover and leave to marinate at room temperature for 10-15 minutes.

2 Meanwhile, thinly slice the red pepper. Thinly slice the spring onions on the diagonal, keeping the white and green parts separate. Peel and segment the oranges, catching the juice in a bowl (there should be 3-4 tablespoons), then cut the segments in half crossways and add them to the bowl.

3 Heat a wok or large, deep sauté pan over moderately high heat until hot. Add the prawns and stir-fry for a few minutes until the prawns turn pink all over. Remove with a slotted spoon and set aside on a plate.

4 Heat the sunflower oil in the pan. Add the red pepper and the white parts of the spring onions and stir-fry for 5 minutes or until softened. Mix in the orange segments and juice, then return the prawns and any juices to the pan and stir until mixed and heated through.

To Serve Taste for seasoning and serve immediately, sprinkled with the green parts of the spring onions.

FISH KEBABS WITH LIME AND ROSEMARY

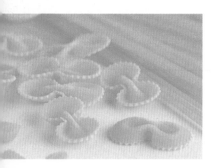

A FRESH AND LIGHT main course, good in summer with a delicate accompaniment such as boiled white rice or new potatoes and a leafy green salad tossed in Curry Lime Vinaigrette (page 188).

4 thick salmon fillets, each weighing 150–175 g (5–6 oz), skinned
salt and freshly ground black pepper

Marinade

2 garlic cloves
1 small fresh rosemary sprig
100 ml (3½ fl oz) olive oil
2 tablespoons lime juice

To Serve

lime slices
2 fresh rosemary sprigs

Serves 4

Preparation time: 5 minutes, plus 10 minutes marinating

Cooking time: 5 minutes

Chef's Tip

You can marinate the fish for slightly longer than 10 minutes if you like, but don't marinate it for longer than 1 hour because the lime juice has the effect of 'cooking' the fish, as in the Mexican raw fish dish called ceviche. There is nothing wrong in this, but the salmon will overcook and become too soft during grilling if it has been marinated for too long.

1   Check the salmon and remove any fine pin bones. Rinse the fish and pat dry. Cut the fish into 2 cm (¾ inch) cubes, place them in a shallow dish and sprinkle with salt and pepper.

2   Make the marinade. Finely chop the garlic and the rosemary leaves. Place in a jug with the olive oil and lime juice and whisk until blended.

3   Pour the marinade over the fish, turn the cubes until they are well coated, then cover and leave to marinate for 10 minutes. Meanwhile, preheat the grill.

4   Thread the cubes of fish on kebab skewers and grill for 5 minutes, turning once. Heat the marinade in a small saucepan.

To Serve Arrange the skewers on warm plates and spoon over the hot marinade. Serve immediately, with the lime slices and rosemary sprigs.

GRILLED FISH WITH MUSTARD BEURRE BLANC

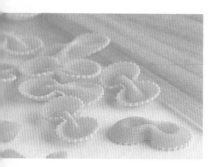

A MAIN COURSE THAT is quintessentially French. The sauce is velvety smooth and rich. Serve with plain vegetables, such as new potatoes and French beans or mangetouts, or follow with a crisp green salad tossed in Vinaigrette (page 188).

8 fish fillets (eg mackerel or trout), each weighing about 90 g (3 oz)
4 tablespoons sunflower oil

Sauce

2 shallots
100 ml (3½ fl oz) dry white wine
1 tablespoon white wine vinegar
100 ml (3½ fl oz) double cream
100 g (3½ oz) cold butter, diced
1 tablespoon wholegrain mustard
salt and freshly ground black pepper

Serves 4

Preparation time: 5 minutes

**Cooking time:
about 15 minutes**

Chef's Tips

Beurre blanc (white butter) is a classic French chef's sauce that is quick and easy to make. It goes well with chicken, vegetables and eggs as well as fish.

Trout fillets are sold in packets at supermarkets. Fresh fillets of mackerel are not always so readily available, but your fishmonger will fillet whole fish for you. For this recipe you will need 4 mackerel.

1 Preheat the grill.

2 Make the sauce. Finely chop the shallots and place them in a saucepan with the wine and vinegar. Bring to the boil, then cook over moderate heat for about 5 minutes until dry. Add the cream, simmer for 2-3 minutes, then whisk in the cold butter a few pieces at a time. Be sure that each batch of butter has completely melted and been whisked in before adding more. Strain the sauce into a warm bowl, stir in the mustard and season to taste. Cover and keep warm.

3 Place the fish fillets on a lightly oiled baking sheet, brush with oil and sprinkle with salt and pepper. Grill for 5-6 minutes.

To Serve Arrange 2 fish fillets on each of 4 warm plates and spoon over the sauce. Serve immediately.

THAI PRAWNS

G ARLICKY AND CHILLI hot, this quick and easy stir-fry makes an impressive supper dish for friends. Have the ingredients prepared before they arrive, then you can toss everything in the wok at the last minute. Serve with jasmine-scented Thai rice.

12 raw jumbo prawns in their shells, thawed if frozen
125 g (4 oz) broccoli florets
1 large red pepper
3–4 garlic cloves
2 tablespoons sunflower oil
1 fresh chilli
3 tablespoons fish sauce
1 tablespoon sugar
freshly ground black pepper
1 small handful of Asian basil, stalks removed

Serves 4

Preparation time: 15 minutes

Cooking time:
10-15 minutes

1   Remove the heads and shells from the prawns, and any black intestinal veins. Wash and dry the prawns and cut them in half if they are very large. Divide the broccoli into tiny sprigs and trim the stalks. Cut the red pepper into thin strips. Crush the garlic finely.

2   Heat the oil in a wok or deep sauté pan over moderate to high heat. Add the garlic and stir-fry until lightly browned, then add the whole chilli and the prawns and stir-fry until the prawns turn pink all over, 3-4 minutes. Remove with a slotted spoon and set aside on a plate.

3   Add the broccoli, red pepper, fish sauce and sugar. Season to taste with pepper and stir-fry for 5-8 minutes until the vegetables are cooked – the broccoli should be bright green and the red pepper just beginning to wilt.

4   Return the prawn mixture to the wok with any juices that have collected on the plate. Add the basil leaves and stir-fry for 1-2 minutes, just long enough to heat the prawns through and let the flavour of the basil infuse.

To Serve   Turn into a warm serving bowl and remove the whole chilli. Serve hot.

Chef's Tips

Fish sauce (nam pla) is an essential flavouring in almost every savoury dish in South-East Asia, especially in Thai cooking. It is a very thin, strong and salty sauce, often combined with sugar in stir-fries. You can get it easily at oriental greengrocers and most large supermarkets, and it keeps almost indefinitely, so is well worth buying.

Fresh Asian basil, also called holy basil, can be bought in bunches in oriental greengrocers. It is more peppery than European sweet basil, but the two are interchangeable in most recipes.

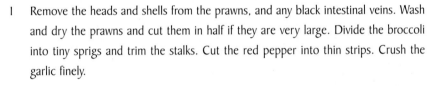

CHICKEN BREASTS WITH WILD MUSHROOMS

T HIS RICH AND CREAMY dish is ideal for a quick after-work supper party. Serve it with fresh pasta such as tagliatelle, or boiled basmati rice. Follow with a mixed salad tossed in Vinaigrette (page 188).

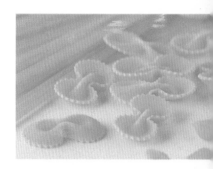

250 g (8 oz) mixed wild mushrooms

3 shallots

1–2 garlic cloves

2 tablespoons sunflower oil

15 g (½ oz) butter

salt and freshly ground black pepper

4 skinless boneless chicken breasts, each weighing about 175 g (6 oz)

300 ml (½ pint) hot chicken stock

175 ml (6 fl oz) double cream

fresh chives, chervil or flat-leaf parsley, to garnish

Serves 4

Preparation time:
10-15 minutes

Cooking time:
about 30 minutes

1 Slice the mushrooms, finely chop the shallots and crush the garlic. Heat the oil and butter in a frying pan. Season the chicken breasts, place them in the pan and cook them over low to moderate heat until they are lightly golden, about 3 minutes on each side.

2 Remove the chicken breasts to a plate and set aside. Add the shallots to the pan and cook, stirring, for 3-5 minutes until softened but not coloured. Add the mushrooms and garlic and toss over moderate to high heat for 2-3 minutes.

3 Pour in the stock and bring to the boil, stirring. Return the chicken to the pan, together with any juices that have collected on the plate, cover and cook over low heat for 10 minutes. Uncover the pan, remove the chicken to the plate again and keep hot.

4 Cook the sauce for another 8-12 minutes over moderate heat, then season to taste and mix in all but about 4 tablespoons of the cream. Return the chicken and any juices to the pan and simmer for another 1-2 minutes, turning once.

To Serve Transfer the chicken to warm plates and spoon the sauce over so that the mushrooms nestle on top of the chicken. Spoon 1 tablespoon cream over each portion, then garnish with herbs. Serve immediately.

Chef's Tip

A mixture of chanterelles, ceps and horns of plenty is a good choice of mushrooms for this dish, but if these are out of season or otherwise unavailable, a mixture of shiitake, oyster and button mushrooms would be equally good. Many supermarkets now sell boxes of mixed wild mushrooms. These are not only convenient but are also good value.

Soft tacos

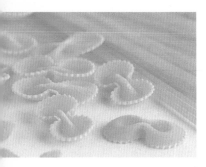

THE WORD 'TACOS' usually conjures up a picture of crisp, deep-fried shells of corn tortillas, stuffed with chilli, refried beans, grated cheese, guacamole, soured cream and the like. This recipe for a simpler, softer version is Californian in style.

375 g (12 oz) rump steak
1 x 35 g sachet taco seasoning mix
1–2 tablespoons sunflower oil
9–12 flour tortillas

Serves 3-4

Preparation time:
20-30 minutes

Cooking time:
about 10 minutes

Accompaniments

1 Spanish onion
2–3 ripe tomatoes
90–125 g (3–4 oz) Cheddar or Monterey Jack cheese
150 ml (¼ pint) soured cream
1 x 125 g tub guacamole

Chef's Tips

Taco seasoning is sold in the Mexican sections of super-markets. The spicy mixture is based on chilli powder, paprika, cumin, garlic and oregano.

Flour tortillas are sold in plastic packets in the bread or Mexican sections. Made from ground corn, they are soft and round like thick pancakes, and have a wonderful earthy flavour.

Variation

Make Quesadillas. Sandwich 2 tortillas with grated cheese, chopped jalapeño chillies and stoned black olives. Heat in a hot non-stick frying pan until the cheese starts to melt. Flip the sandwich over and heat the other side.

1   Cut the rump steak into thin strips, trimming off excess fat and any sinew. Put the strips in a bowl and sprinkle them with the taco seasoning. Stir the strips to coat them in the seasoning, then set aside.

2   Prepare the accompaniments. Finely chop the onion and tomatoes and grate the cheese. Place in separate small bowls. Spoon the soured cream and guacamole into separate small bowls.

3   Heat the oil in a frying pan until hot. Add the steak strips and fry over moderate to high heat until cooked to your liking, 5-8 minutes. Tip into a serving bowl and keep hot.

4   Dry-fry the tortillas in a non-stick frying pan for a few seconds on each side until they puff up.

To Serve Let each person make their own tacos – the guacamole is usually spread over the tortilla, the beef sprinkled over and topped with onion, tomatoes, cheese and soured cream. Once filled, the tortilla can be rolled up or folded over like an envelope. Tacos are always eaten with the hands.

CHILLI

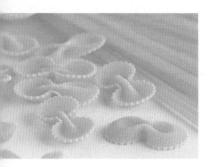

Serves 2-3

Preparation time: 5 minutes

**Cooking time:
about 25 minutes**

Chef's Tips

There are many types of chilli powder. Most of them are not pure chilli, but a ready mix of the traditional spices and herbs used in chilli con carne — sometimes called chilli seasoning. Check the label for chilli strength before you buy, because some brands are fiery hot. The quantity here is for a medium strength powder, so you may need to add more or less.

The chilli will keep for 3 days in the refrigerator, or it can be frozen for up to 3 months. When you reheat it, add a little hot water to prevent it sticking to the pan, and make sure it is bubbling well for 10 minutes.

YOU CAN MAKE a batch of chilli in 30 minutes, and any leftovers reheat well the next day. In fact, it tastes even better after standing and reheating. Serve it over boiled rice and top with grated Cheddar cheese and soured cream.

1 onion
2 garlic cloves
1 red pepper
2 tablespoons sunflower oil
400 g (14 oz) ground or minced beef
2 teaspoons chilli powder
1 x 400 g can red kidney or pinto beans
1 x 400 g can chopped tomatoes
salt and freshly ground black pepper

1   Finely chop the onion and garlic, keeping them separate. Dice the red pepper. Heat the oil in a saucepan, add the onion and cook over low heat until translucent. Add the garlic and red pepper and cook for 1 minute.

2   Add the beef and cook until browned, stirring constantly and pressing with the back of the spoon to remove any lumps. Add the chilli powder and stir for 1–2 minutes.

3   Drain and rinse the beans, then add to the pan with the tomatoes. Stir well, season to taste and simmer for 20 minutes.

To Serve   Taste for seasoning and serve hot.

BEEF WITH BROCCOLI

A N AUTHENTIC CHINESE stir-fry that takes only minutes to cook if you get everything prepared beforehand. Serve with boiled rice or egg noodles for a midweek meal to share with friends.

500–625 g (1–1¼ lb) rump, sirloin or fillet steak
½ teaspoon salt
1 tablespoon rice wine or sherry
3 tablespoons soy sauce
1 tablespoon cornflour
175 g (6 oz) broccoli florets
1 medium yellow or red onion
2 garlic cloves
4 tablespoons groundnut oil
1 tablespoon sugar
2 tablespoons oyster sauce

Serves 3-4

Preparation time: 25 minutes

Cooking time:
about 10 minutes

1   Trim the meat of any excess fat or gristle. With the knife at a 45° angle to the cutting board, cut the meat into thin slices. Place the meat in a bowl and add the salt, rice wine or sherry and 1 tablespoon of the soy sauce. Sprinkle with the cornflour and mix everything together well. Cover and set aside for 15 minutes.

2   Meanwhile, divide the broccoli into tiny sprigs and trim the stalks. Cut the onion lengthways into eighths. Crush the garlic.

3   Heat 2 tablespoons of the oil in a wok or deep sauté pan until very hot. Add the beef and stir-fry over high heat for 2-3 minutes. Remove with a slotted spoon and set aside on a plate. Turn the heat down to low, add the remaining oil to the wok, then add the broccoli and 4 tablespoons water. Cover immediately and allow the broccoli to steam for 2 minutes.

4   Uncover, add the onion, garlic and remaining soy sauce and stir-fry over high heat for 1-2 minutes or until the liquid has evaporated. Return the beef to the wok with any juices that have collected on the plate, stir well, then sprinkle with the sugar and oyster sauce. Stir-fry for 1-2 minutes until all the ingredients are well blended.

To Serve   Turn into a warm serving bowl and serve immediately.

Chef's Tips

To save preparation time, you can buy ready sliced beef for stir-fries in some supermarkets.

Groundnut or peanut oil is often used in stir-fries because it can be heated to a high temperature without burning. Some supermarkets sell bottles of 'stir-fry oil', a mixture of vegetable oil and sesame oil flavoured with ginger and garlic. This would also be ideal for this dish. Never use sesame oil on its own for stir-frying: it has a low smoke point and burns easily.

Variation

Instead of the broccoli, you can use 2 red or orange peppers, cut into thin strips.

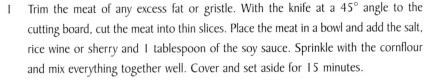

STEAK WITH GREEN PEPPERCORN SAUCE

Serves 2

Preparation time:
7-10 minutes

Cooking time:
about 20 minutes

Chef's Tip

Whole green peppercorns are sold in small jars or bottles in delicatessens and supermarkets. Once the jar or bottle has been opened, they will keep in the refrigerator for several months. They are softer than dried peppercorns, but still have quite a crunchy bite to them, so are almost always crushed before use.

A CLASSIC FRENCH bistro-style dish. Serve with pommes allumettes (French fries), which can be cooking in the oven while you are preparing and cooking the steaks. Add a salad garnish if you like.

2 small shallots
30 g (1 oz) green peppercorns in brine
45 g (1½ oz) butter
200 ml (7 fl oz) hot beef stock
90 ml (3 fl oz) double cream
salt and freshly ground black pepper
2 fillet steaks
2 teaspoons sunflower oil
2 tablespoons brandy (optional)

1 Finely chop the shallots. Drain the peppercorns well, then crush them with a fork. In a saucepan, melt 30 g (1 oz) of the butter, add the shallots and cook over low heat for 2-3 minutes. Take care not to let the shallots colour. Add the peppercorns and cook for 2 minutes.

2 Add the stock, bring to the boil and cook for 5-10 minutes or until reduced by about half. Add the cream and simmer for 5 minutes. Add salt to taste and set aside.

3 Heat a frying pan over moderate heat. Season the steaks with salt and pepper. Add the oil and remaining butter to the hot pan and heat them until the butter is foaming. Add the steaks and cook them for 2-4 minutes on each side, according to how you like them. Transfer the steaks to a plate and keep warm.

4 Pour off and discard the fat from the pan, then return the pan to the heat. Add the steaks, then the brandy (if using) and the sauce. Cook for 30 seconds on each side.

To Serve Transfer the steaks to warm plates, spoon the peppercorn sauce over them and serve immediately.

GRILLED LAMB CUTLETS WITH CORN AND PEPPER SALSA

THE COMBINATION OF sizzling hot cutlets with a cool and refreshing salsa is simply sensational. For a dish that is both colourful and tasty, serve with baby new potatoes tossed in butter and chopped fresh herbs.

6 lamb cutlets (best end of neck)
2 garlic cloves
1 fresh thyme sprig
4 tablespoons olive oil
salt and freshly ground black pepper

Salsa

1 red pepper
1 garlic clove
1 large handful of fresh coriander
1 x 198 g can sweetcorn
4 tablespoons olive oil
1 tablespoon lime juice
pinch of sugar

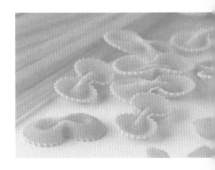

Serves 2

Preparation time: 20 minutes

Cooking time: 6-8 minutes, or a few minutes longer

1   Trim off any excess fat from the cutlets, then place in a shallow dish. Chop the garlic and thyme leaves, place them in a bowl and mix in the olive oil and pepper to taste. Brush over both sides of the cutlets. Set aside for about 20 minutes.

2   Meanwhile, preheat the grill and make the salsa. Finely dice the red pepper and chop the garlic and coriander. Drain the sweetcorn, place in a bowl and add the red pepper, garlic, coriander, olive oil, lime juice and sugar. Mix well and add salt and pepper to taste.

3   Cook the cutlets under the hot grill for 3-4 minutes on each side or until they are done to your liking.

To Serve Place 3 cutlets on each warm plate and spoon some of the salsa alongside. Serve immediately, with the remaining salsa handed separately.

Chef's Tip

Best end of neck cutlets have a tender and juicy 'eye' of meat, and they cook in next to no time. They are sold in packets in supermarkets, sometimes with the ends of the bones trimmed off. If you like lamb chump chops, these can also be cooked in the same way, allowing a few minutes' extra cooking time.

Paella

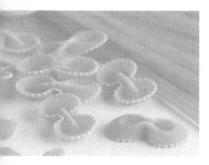

An ALL-IN-ONE dish that is good for an informal midweek supper with friends. Serve with crusty bread and a Spanish-style salad of sliced tomatoes, raw onion rings and chopped garlic with olive oil, lemon juice and salt and pepper.

Serves 3-4

Preparation time: 15 minutes

Cooking time:
about 35 minutes

1 pinch of saffron threads
2 skinless boneless chicken breasts
1 medium onion
1 medium green pepper
1–2 garlic cloves, to taste
12 large fresh mussels
2 tablespoons olive oil
200 g (7 oz) long grain rice
750 ml (1¼ pints) hot chicken stock or water
salt and freshly ground black pepper
3–4 raw tiger king prawns in their shells, thawed if frozen
chopped fresh flat-leaf parsley, to garnish

Chef's Tip

In Spain, paella is usually made with a short grain rice, which gives a sticky consistency similar to that of risotto. Long grain rice is easier to use because it can be left unattended for longer without sticking. If you like, you can use easy-cook long grain rice. This has polished grains to prevent it from sticking.

1 Soak the saffron threads in 1 tablespoon hot water. Meanwhile, cut the chicken into 1.25 cm (½ inch) cubes or little-finger-sized strips. Finely slice the onion and green pepper. Crush the garlic. Scrub and rinse the mussels.

2 Heat the oil in a deep sauté pan or flameproof casserole. Add the chicken and toss over moderate to high heat for about 2 minutes until all of the pieces have turned white. Remove to a plate.

3 Add the onion and sauté over low heat until soft and light golden. Add the rice, green pepper and garlic and cook, stirring, for 1 minute until well coated with oil. Add 600 ml (1 pint) of the stock or water, the saffron and its liquid and salt and pepper. Stir until boiling, then cover and cook over low heat for 10 minutes.

4 Add the chicken and remaining stock or water. Stir to mix well. Place the mussels and prawns on top of the rice, cover tightly and cook for a further 10 minutes.

To Serve Uncover the pan and check that all of the mussels have opened. Discard any that are closed. Sprinkle with chopped parsley and serve hot.

CREOLE JAMBALAYA

SPICY AND HOT, this chicken, rice and prawn dish comes from the Caribbean. It is perfect for midweek entertaining because it can be partially prepared the night before. The flavour improves with standing and reheating.

1 small onion
1 green pepper
4 celery sticks
4 garlic cloves
100 g (3½ oz) butter
1 teaspoon cayenne pepper
1 bay leaf
2 fresh thyme sprigs
1 teaspoon dried oregano
salt and freshly ground black pepper
1 x 700–800 g can whole peeled tomatoes
375 ml (12 fl oz) hot chicken or vegetable stock
8 skinless chicken thighs
175 g (6 oz) long grain rice
250 g (8 oz) cooked and peeled tiger king prawns, thawed if frozen
fresh thyme leaves, to garnish

Serves 4

Preparation time: 10 minutes

Cooking time:
about 45 minutes

1   Finely chop the onion, green pepper, celery and garlic, in a food processor if you have one. Melt the butter in a large flameproof casserole and sauté the chopped vegetables over low to moderate heat until soft and lightly coloured.

2   Add the cayenne, herbs and salt and pepper to taste. Stir for 1-2 minutes, then add the tomatoes and stock and simmer for 10 minutes, stirring frequently. Add the chicken, cover and simmer for 20 minutes.

3   Add the rice and stir to mix, then cover and cook for 15 minutes, stirring occasionally. Place the prawns on top of the jambalaya, cover and heat through for 2-3 minutes.

To Serve Taste for seasoning and serve hot, sprinkled with fresh thyme leaves.

Chef's Tips

Chicken thighs are sold in packets in most supermarkets. They have moist, tender meat that is better for casseroles and stews than breast meat, which tends to be dry if cooked too long. Bone-in thighs are the most succulent, but if you prefer you can buy boneless thighs and cut the meat into chunks.

To prepare ahead, cook up to the end of step 2, leave to cool, then refrigerate. About 20 minutes before serving, bring to a simmer, then continue with the recipe.

After work
quick and easy ideas

Fish Fillets and Steaks

- Top fish with shredded fresh root ginger and lemon grass, julienned vegetables, crème fraîche, grated lemon rind and chopped fresh parsley or coriander. Wrap in foil and bake in the oven.

- Pan-fry salmon fillets in oil and butter. Make a simple noisette butter. Deglaze pan with lemon juice, swirl in a knob of butter and stir over high heat until foaming and turning colour. Season and pour over salmon. Serve with lemon wedges.

- Grill fish and serve topped with Maître d'Hôtel Butter (page 187).

- Or serve with anchovy butter. Mash canned anchovies, beat into softened unsalted butter and season with a few drops of lemon juice and black pepper. Tapenade (anchovy and olive paste) can be used instead of anchovies.

- Or mix softened butter with grated rind and juice of lemon or orange and salt and pepper. If using orange, add 1 teaspoon sun-dried tomato paste or tomato purée.

- If you prefer, pan-fry fish and remove, then add flavoured butter to pan, let it sizzle, then pour over fish.

Chicken Breasts

- Pan-fry skinless boneless whole breasts or strips in olive oil or oil and butter. Deglaze pan with 1-2 tablespoons each balsamic vinegar and orange or lemon juice. Drizzle over chicken and sprinkle with chopped fresh sage, rosemary or thyme.

- For a rich sauce, stir a little crème fraîche or double cream into the pan juices.

- For a sweet and sour sauce, add a pinch or two of sugar.

- For a Mediterranean flavour, add a few black olives, stoned and sliced or roughly chopped, or a few thinly sliced sun-dried tomatoes or roasted peppers.

- Split whole breasts lengthways and fill with pesto, then pan-fry in olive oil for 15 minutes, turning once. Deglaze pan with water, wine or Marsala.

- Season skinless boneless whole breasts, wrap in Parma ham and place in an oiled baking dish. Top with slices of cheese and bake at 200°C (400°F) Gas 6 for 20 minutes. If available, wrap 1-2 fresh sage or basil leaves between chicken and ham, or spread top of chicken with pesto or Roasted Garlic flesh (page 184).

- Marinate whole breasts (with skin) or strips in Teriyaki Marinade (page 186) for at least 10-20 minutes. Grill whole breasts, brushing frequently with the marinade. Stir-fry strips in a hot wok.

Pork Chops and Steaks

- Spread with Maître d'Hôtel Butter (page 187) made with sage. Grill on one side. Turn pork over, spread with more butter and continue grilling.

- Serve topped with a cold salsa of finely chopped onion, garlic, tomato, mango or papaya and chilli, tossed with lime juice, chopped fresh coriander and salt and pepper.

- Mix crunchy wholegrain mustard into butter and spread over pork. Grill as above and serve with Corn Salad (page 150).

- Pan-fry pork in sunflower oil and butter. Deglaze pan with pineapple juice, honey, wine vinegar and soy sauce. Pour over pork.

- Or deglaze pan with orange juice, a little marmalade and a pinch of ground coriander or cinnamon.

- Or deglaze with orange juice, wholegrain mustard and brown sugar.

- Add a dash of sherry, Madeira, vermouth or white wine if you have a bottle open.

- Or deglaze pan with cider and add thin slices of unpeeled dessert apple. Soften for a few minutes and pour over pork. The addition of cream or crème fraîche will make it porc à la normande.

Lamb Chops and Cutlets

- Marinate in Spiced Yogurt Marinade (page 186) for at least 10-20 minutes. Grill and serve with Cucumber and Mint Raita (page 152). Or make an even quicker raita: stir 1-2 tablespoons mint jelly into a carton of Greek yogurt.

- Spread lamb with Snail Butter (page 187). Grill on one side. Turn lamb over, spread with more butter and continue grilling.

- Or use chutney butter, a classic with lamb. Pound chutney of your choice with a mortar and pestle and mix into softened butter.

- Pan-fry lamb in olive oil. Deglaze pan with white wine, lemon juice and chopped fresh rosemary. Add chopped garlic if you like, and a splash of Pernod if you have some handy.

- Pan-fry lamb in olive oil. Deglaze pan with Madeira, port or sherry, add chopped fresh tarragon, crème fraîche and salt and pepper. Reduce, pour over lamb and top with fresh tarragon. If you like, add a few capers to the sauce.

- Pan-fry lamb. Deglaze pan with red wine, redcurrant jelly and salt and pepper. If you like, add a few crushed juniper berries.

Beef Steaks

- Pan-fry seasoned steaks in butter and oil. Remove and keep hot. Deglaze pan with sugar, red wine and garlic, then pour over the steaks.

- Spread steaks with Roasted Red Pepper Butter (page 187). Grill on one side. Turn steaks over, spread with more butter and continue grilling.

- Grill steaks or chargrill them in a ridged cast iron pan. Stir bottled grated horseradish or wasabi (Japanese horseradish) into crème fraîche and serve on the side.

- Or make a simple soubise sauce. Caramelize thinly sliced onions by cooking them for 15 minutes in olive oil with stock, sugar, salt and pepper. Pile on top of grilled steaks.

- Make a simple steak au poivre. Crush black peppercorns coarsely with a mortar and pestle. Brush steaks with oil and press peppercorns all over. Grill to your liking.

Weekend Entertaining

MOST OF US have a little more time to spare at the weekend than during the week, and the recipes in this chapter have been chosen with this in mind. You may have invited friends for a Saturday dinner party, family for a special Sunday lunch, or a few people round for an informal soirée or al fresco lunch in the garden. Maybe you plan an intimate dinner for two or, at the other extreme, you may have a houseful of guests for the whole weekend. These are very different occasions, but for all of them you will need to plan, shop, prepare and cook more than usual.

The recipes in this chapter are easy, but the results are sensational. They are all main courses, arranged according to their main ingredient – fish and shellfish, chicken and duck, beef, lamb and pork. Some are light and simple, some rich and creamy, others hearty and substantial. There is a wide choice of flavours, a fusion of French, Italian and Scandinavian favourites with spicy ethnic specialities from China, India, Thailand and the Middle East. There is also a selection of menu ideas on pages 124-125. These will help you put main course dishes together with recipes from elsewhere in the book.

Read your chosen recipes through carefully and prepare and assemble the ingredients before starting to cook. In the long run, this will save you time. All of the ingredients are easy to find in the supermarket or local delicatessen. Preparation and cooking times are kept to a minimum, and each recipe gives you serving ideas and tips to make it easy for you once guests have arrived. Plan your occasion well in advance and make a timetable of what you have to do and when, working backwards from serving time. Don't forget to build in extra time for drinks and nibbles before the meal – and the possibility of someone arriving late. This way you can make every special occasion relaxed, for both you and your guests.

Seafood Fricassee

RICH, CREAMY AND luxurious, this is a main course for a very special dinner party. The chefs in Paris serve it in a copper chafing dish and it looks sensational. Serve with plain boiled rice, and follow with a salad.

1 kg (2 lb) large mussels
500 g (1 lb) skinless salmon fillet
12 large scallops
2 shallots
1 large handful of fresh flat-leaf parsley
1 fresh thyme sprig
1 bay leaf
400 ml (14 fl oz) dry white wine
12 large raw Mediterranean prawns in their shells
400 ml (14 fl oz) double cream
salt and freshly ground black pepper

Serves 4-6

Preparation time: 45 minutes

Cooking time:
about 20 minutes

Variations

For garlic lovers, add 2-4 chopped garlic cloves with the herbs at the beginning.

For a hint of spice, sweat the shallots in 20 g (¾ oz) butter with 1-2 teaspoons curry powder or garam masala before adding the wine.

1   Scrub the mussels well and remove any beards and barnacles with a small sharp knife. Discard any mussels that are open or do not close when tapped sharply against the work surface. Cut the salmon into 2.5 cm (1 inch) cubes. Separate the corals from the scallops, then cut off and discard the rubbery muscles. Cut the scallops in half. Finely chop the shallots. Separate the parsley leaves from the stalks and chop the leaves.

2   Put the shallots, parsley stalks, thyme, bay leaf and wine in a large saucepan and boil over high heat until reduced by about half. Add the mussels and prawns, cover and cook over moderate heat until the mussels open and the prawns are pink, about 5 minutes. Remove the mussels and prawns with a slotted spoon. Shell the prawns.

3   Strain the liquid through a fine sieve into a clean pan and bring to the boil. Reduce the heat to low, add the scallops, corals and salmon, cover and cook for 3 minutes only. Remove the fish and shellfish with a slotted spoon.

4   Reduce the liquid until syrupy, add the cream and simmer until the sauce coats the back of a spoon. Season well. Add the salmon, scallops and prawns, shake to coat in the sauce, then arrange the mussels on top. Cover and heat gently for 2-3 minutes.

To Serve Sprinkle with the chopped parsley and serve immediately.

SPICED PRAWNS WITH SWEET AND SOUR SAUCE

Serves 2-6

Preparation time: 10 minutes

Cooking time:
about 15 minutes

Variations

Langoustines or strips of white fish, chicken or pork can be used instead of the prawns.

Ready made garam masala can be used instead of the five-spice powder.

THIS CHINESE RECIPE is simple as well as quick. For a special meal for two, serve it with boiled or steamed rice or stir-fried vegetables. With other dishes as part of a Chinese meal, it is enough to serve 4-6 people.

20 raw tiger king prawns, peeled and deveined
1 tablespoon five-spice powder
1 large egg
2 tablespoons cornflour
about 600 ml (1 pint) groundnut oil for deep-frying

Sauce

1½ teaspoons cornflour
3 tablespoons light malt vinegar
3 tablespoons sugar
3 tablespoons tomato ketchup
1 tablespoon soy sauce
pinch of salt

1   Sprinkle the prawns with the spice powder and set aside. Beat the egg in a bowl, add the cornflour and beat well to make a batter. Mix together all the ingredients for the sauce in a small saucepan. Stir until smooth.

2   Heat the oil in a wok until very hot but not smoking. Dip about one-quarter of the prawns in the batter, then deep-fry them in the hot oil for 2-3 minutes until golden. Remove with a slotted spoon. Drain and keep hot on kitchen paper. Repeat with the remaining prawns and batter.

3   Bring the sauce to the boil, stirring. Add a little water to thin it to a runny consistency and stir vigorously.

To Serve Arrange the prawns on warm plates, spoon the sauce alongside and serve immediately.

SCALLOPS WITH TOMATO AND SAFFRON

A SIMPLE DISH THAT can be made very quickly at short notice – good for an informal supper party. Fresh scallops are best, but you can use frozen ones as long as they are thoroughly thawed and dried before cooking.

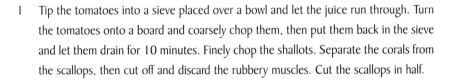

1 x 700–800 g can whole peeled tomatoes
2–3 shallots
20 large scallops
90 ml (3 fl oz) olive oil
salt and freshly ground black pepper
1 large pinch of saffron threads or 1 sachet saffron powder
125 ml (4 fl oz) dry white wine

Serves 4

Preparation time: 10 minutes

Cooking time:
about 25 minutes

1   Tip the tomatoes into a sieve placed over a bowl and let the juice run through. Turn the tomatoes onto a board and coarsely chop them, then put them back in the sieve and let them drain for 10 minutes. Finely chop the shallots. Separate the corals from the scallops, then cut off and discard the rubbery muscles. Cut the scallops in half.

2   Heat 2 tablespoons of the oil in a frying pan over moderate to high heat. Season the scallops and sear them for 1 minute on each side in the hot oil. Transfer them to a plate with a slotted spoon.

3   Add the shallots to the pan and cook for 1 minute. Pour in the liquid from the tomatoes, add the saffron and cook over moderate heat for 5-8 minutes or until the liquid has reduced by about half. Set aside.

4   In a separate pan, cook the tomatoes and wine in the remaining oil over moderate heat until thick, 5-10 minutes. Season well to taste, then add the saffron sauce and scallops. Cook for 2 minutes only, just until very hot.

To Serve   Taste for seasoning, then spoon over hot boiled rice or pasta.

Variations

For additional flavour, fry some chopped bacon or sliced button mushrooms with the shallots.

Use cubes of monkfish fillet or large raw Mediterranean or tiger king prawns instead of scallops.

FISH SOUP

THIS IS A very special main-meal soup with a delicate but absolutely delicious flavour. Serve it for a Scandinavian-style Sunday lunch or supper party. It can be spooned over boiled rice in deep soup plates, or served solo with crusty French bread.

1 small onion

2 small carrots

2 medium leeks (white and pale green leaves only)

15 g (½ oz) butter

1 tablespoon olive oil

250 ml (8 fl oz) dry white wine

1 large pinch of saffron threads or 1 sachet saffron powder

salt and freshly ground black pepper

500 g (1 lb) skinless thick cod or haddock fillet

500 g (1 lb) skinless thick salmon fillet

6-8 large scallops

250 g (8 oz) raw peeled tiger king prawns, thawed if frozen

To Serve

2 tablespoons chopped fresh dill

4 tablespoons cream or crème fraîche

Serves 4

Preparation time:
15-20 minutes

Cooking time: 35 minutes

1   Thinly slice the onion, carrots and leeks. Melt the butter with the oil in a large saucepan or flameproof casserole. Add the sliced vegetables, cover and cook over low heat for 15 minutes. Stir occasionally during this time.

2   Stir in the wine and bubble briskly until evaporated, then add 900 ml (1½ pints) water and the saffron. Bring to the boil. Season, cover and simmer for 15 minutes.

3   Cut the white fish and salmon into 5 cm (2 inch) cubes. Separate the corals from the scallops, then cut off and discard the rubbery muscles. Cut the scallops in half. Add the white fish and salmon to the soup and barely simmer for 3 minutes. Add the prawns, scallops and corals and simmer for 3 minutes only.

To Serve   Sprinkle in half the dill and add the cream. Shake the pan gently to mix without breaking up the fish. Serve hot, sprinkled with the remaining dill.

Chef's Tip

This is the perfect dish for entertaining because the cooking liquid actually improves in flavour if made the day before. Cook it up to the end of step 2, let it cool, then cover and refrigerate overnight. Before serving, all you need to do is bring the liquid to simmering point and continue from the beginning of step 3.

MONKFISH WITH OLIVE AND TOMATO SAUCE

A SOPHISTICATED DISH MADE simple by using ready prepared ingredients from the supermarket. Serve it for a maximum of 4 people – any more than this and you will find the last-minute cooking and serving difficult to manage.

625 g (1¼ lb) monkfish fillets
2 tablespoons plain flour
salt and freshly ground black pepper
2 ripe tomatoes
1 tablespoon extra-virgin olive oil
2 tablespoons chopped fresh flat-leaf parsley or coriander
pinch of sugar
375 g (12 oz) prepared cabbage
90 g (3 oz) butter
4 tablespoons bottled olive and tomato sauce
90 ml (3 fl oz) dry white wine or water

Serves 4

Preparation time: 20 minutes

Cooking time:
about 15 minutes

Chef's Tips

Olive and tomato sauce is sold in small jars like pesto. It is available in supermarkets and delicatessens, and makes an excellent sauce for pasta, chicken, steaks and chops as well as fish. Once the jar is opened, it keeps for 2 weeks in the refrigerator, so it is well worth buying.

Bags of ready prepared greens are sold in the fresh chilled cabinets. They are washed and ready to cook, often with the leaves cut up or shredded into ribbons (as called for in this recipe), so they save an immense amount of time.

1   Trim the monkfish if necessary, cut into 16 medallions and coat in the flour seasoned with salt and pepper. Peel the tomatoes and cut them in half. Squeeze out the seeds, then dice the flesh finely. Place in a bowl and mix with the olive oil, half the herbs, the sugar and salt and pepper to taste. Cover and refrigerate. Cut the cabbage into ribbons if this has not already been done.

2   Melt 60 g (2 oz) of the butter in a large sauté pan until foaming. Add the monkfish and sauté over moderate to high heat for 3 minutes on each side until golden and just cooked through. Remove with a slotted spoon and keep hot.

3   Melt the remaining butter in the pan, add the cabbage and salt and pepper to taste and stir-fry over high heat for 3-4 minutes or until wilted. Remove with a slotted spoon and arrange in the centre of 4 warm plates. Keep hot.

4   Add the sauce to the pan with the wine or water. Stir to mix and bring to the boil. Lower the heat, stir in the remaining herbs, then return the monkfish to the pan and quickly coat with the sauce.

To Serve   Arrange 4 medallions on each mound of cabbage, spooning the sauce over them. Spoon a little of the tomato mixture in the centre and serve immediately.

BAKED FISH WITH GINGER AND RICE WINE

W ITH ITS SUBTLE oriental flavour, this very quick Chinese dish will certainly inspire compliments. Serve with bowls of boiled or steamed rice and colourful and crisp stir-fried vegetables.

5 cm (2 inch) piece of fresh root ginger
4 spring onions
1 tablespoon sesame oil
salt and freshly ground black pepper
4 star anise
4 thick fish fillets, each weighing about 150 g (5 oz)
125 ml (4 fl oz) rice wine

1   Preheat the oven to 220°C (425°F) Gas 7. Peel and grate the ginger. Thinly slice the spring onions on the diagonal. Brush the bottom of a roasting tin with the sesame oil and sprinkle with salt and pepper.

2   Place the star anise in the tin, spacing them well, and place 1 fish fillet on top of each. Sprinkle with the ginger and spring onions. Pour the rice wine over and around the fish.

3   Place the tin on the hob. Bring the wine to the boil, then cover the tin tightly with foil and put in the oven. Bake for about 10 minutes until the fish flakes easily when tested with the tip of a sharp knife. The exact cooking time will depend on the fish and the size of the fillets.

To Serve   Lift the fish out of the tin with a fish slice and place on warm plates. Spoon the juices and flavourings around and serve immediately.

Serves 4

Preparation time: 10 minutes

Cooking time:
about 15 minutes

Chef's Tips

Any boneless fish fillets can be used. Cod, haddock, brill, sea bass, mullet or monkfish are all suitable, depending on your budget and the season. Leave the skin on the fish, so that it retains its shape.

Frozen root ginger is much easier to grate than fresh, so keep a packet of it in the freezer. It will thaw instantly when it is grated.

SOLE WITH SMOKED SALMON

T HIS IS AN impressive and elegant dish for a special dinner party. Serve it with a plain accompaniment such as boiled new potatoes tossed with butter and chopped fresh herbs, and a simple green vegetable like courgettes or mangetouts.

2 large shallots
a knob of softened butter
salt and freshly ground black pepper
12 sole fillets, skinned
4–6 tablespoons finely chopped fresh herbs
150–175 g (5–6 oz) sliced smoked salmon
400 ml (14 fl oz) dry white wine
400 ml (14 fl oz) double cream
fresh herbs, to garnish

Serves 4-6

Preparation time: 30 minutes

Cooking time:
about 20 minutes

1   Preheat the oven to 180°C (350°F) Gas 4. Finely chop the shallots. Brush the inside of a large flameproof casserole with butter, then sprinkle with the chopped shallots and a little salt and pepper.

2   Trim off any ragged edges from the sole. Using the flat of a large chef's knife, lightly pound each fillet on the skinned side. Sprinkle this same side with pepper and herbs.

3   Cut the smoked salmon into narrow strips and fit them on top of the sole fillets, over the herbs. Roll up each fillet from the broadest end and secure with a wooden toothpick. Stand the rolls upright in the prepared casserole, pour the wine over and bring to the boil over moderate heat. Quickly cover with buttered baking parchment or foil, then the casserole lid. Cook in the oven for 12 minutes.

4   Remove the fish with a slotted spoon, cover with the parchment or foil and keep hot. Place the casserole on the hob and bring the cooking liquid to the boil. Add the cream and boil, stirring, until reduced to your liking. Taste for seasoning.

To Serve   Remove the toothpicks from the fish and arrange the fish rolls on warm plates. Spoon the sauce over and garnish with fresh herbs. Serve immediately.

Chef's Tip

Supermarkets and fishmongers sell individual sole fillets, but if you have to ask for whole fish to be filleted you will need 3 whole fish to get 12 fillets. Buy lemon sole (it is less expensive than Dover sole) and ask the fishmonger to remove the skin.

GRILLED RED MULLET NIÇOISE

A LOVELY LIGHT DISH to serve on a summer's evening – preferably outside so you can smell the fish cooking on the barbecue. The sauce has an exquisite Provençal flavour from the tomatoes, garlic, anchovies and black olives.

4 ripe tomatoes, total weight about 375 g (12 oz)

1 garlic clove

5 black olives

4 tablespoons olive oil

2–4 drained canned anchovy fillets

30 g (1 oz) butter, softened

freshly ground black pepper

1 tablespoon capers (optional)

4 fresh red mullet, each weighing about 250 g (8 oz)

2 fresh herbs sprigs (basil, rosemary or thyme), to garnish

Serves 2

Preparation time:
10-15 minutes

Cooking time:
about 25 minutes

1   Peel the tomatoes and cut them in half. Squeeze out the seeds, then dice the flesh. Finely chop the garlic. Stone the olives and cut each one in half or into quarters. Heat 2 tablespoons of the olive oil in a saucepan over moderate heat. Add the tomatoes and garlic and simmer for 10-15 minutes or until most of the liquid has evaporated. Meanwhile, light the barbecue or preheat the grill.

2   Using a fork, mash the anchovies with the butter. Off the heat, stir the anchovy butter into the tomatoes. Season with pepper and stir in the olives and capers (if using). Keep hot.

3   Make 3 diagonal slashes on either side of each red mullet. Brush with the remaining olive oil and season with salt and pepper. Barbecue or grill for 2-3 minutes on each side.

To Serve Spoon the tomato mixture onto warm plates and arrange the fish on top or to the side. Garnish with a sprig of fresh herbs and serve immediately, with a fresh baguette and a well-chilled dry white or rosé wine.

Chef's Tips

Finely chopped fresh basil, rosemary or thyme can be added to the tomatoes.

The sauce can be made ahead of time and quickly reheated just before serving.

Whole fresh red mullet are not always available. Frozen red mullet fillets can be used instead – allow 6 fillets for 2 people, thaw them and barbecue or grill for only 1-2 minutes on each side.

CHICKEN TAGINE

Serves 4

Preparation time: 15 minutes

Cooking time:
about 1¼ hours

Chef's Tips

A whole chicken is normally used to make tagine, but pieces are easier to serve. For convenience, ask your butcher to joint the chicken for you, or buy pieces from the supermarket. Legs and thighs are best for stews like this.

Pickled lemons are used in tagines for their sharp and salty citrus tang, but they are not essential. You may find them in a Middle Eastern or North African grocer, or you can make them using the recipe on page 185. An alternative is to buy a bottle of preserved lemon slices in lemon juice. Although not authentic, they do add the required touch of sourness. They are available at most supermarkets.

S PICY MOROCCAN TAGINE is a good dish for an informal supper party. Here it is made with tangy olives and lemons. Potatoes are included in the stew, so no accompaniment is needed, but a refreshing cucumber or tomato salad would be nice to follow.

2 onions
2 garlic cloves
500 g (1 lb) peeled new potatoes
1 chicken, cut into 8 serving pieces
salt and freshly ground black pepper
3 tablespoons olive oil
1 tablespoon ground cumin
1 teaspoon ground ginger
1 teaspoon paprika
1 large pinch of saffron threads or 1 sachet saffron powder
about 500 ml (16 fl oz) hot chicken stock
2–3 pieces of pickled lemon (optional)
60–90 g (2–3 oz) stoned black olives
chopped fresh coriander or flat-leaf parsley, to garnish

1   Finely slice the onions. Crush the garlic. Cut the potatoes into halves or quarters if large. Remove the skin from the chicken and sprinkle the chicken with salt and pepper.

2   Heat the oil in a large flameproof casserole. Place half the chicken pieces in the hot oil and fry until browned on all sides. Remove and repeat with the remaining chicken.

3   Return all the chicken pieces to the pan and add the onions, garlic and spices. Stir until the chicken pieces are well coated, then pour in enough stock to just cover them. Bring to the boil, cover and simmer gently for 30 minutes.

4   Roughly chop the pickled lemon pieces (if using) and add to the tagine with the potatoes and olives. Cover and cook for a further 30 minutes or until both the chicken and potatoes are tender.

To Serve Taste the sauce for seasoning and serve the tagine hot, sprinkled with chopped coriander or parsley.

THAI CHICKEN WITH PEPPERS

HAI INGREDIENTS AND French culinary techniques fuse harmoniously in this delicately presented dish. Its flavour is superb and needs no embellishment, so serve it very simply, with jasmine-scented Thai rice.

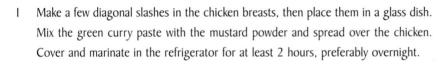

4 skinless boneless chicken breasts
4–6 tablespoons green Thai curry paste
1 tablespoon English mustard powder
1 large onion
2 peppers (green and red)
2 tablespoons groundnut oil
30 g (1 oz) butter
pinch of salt
200 ml (7 fl oz) hot chicken stock
5 tablespoons warm sesame oil
2 tablespoons peanut butter

Serves 4

Preparation time: 20 minutes, plus marinating

Cooking time: about 30 minutes

1   Make a few diagonal slashes in the chicken breasts, then place them in a glass dish. Mix the green curry paste with the mustard powder and spread over the chicken. Cover and marinate in the refrigerator for at least 2 hours, preferably overnight.

2   Finely slice the onion and cut the peppers into very thin strips. Heat the oil and butter in a frying pan, add the chicken and fry over low to moderate heat for 7 minutes on each side or until lightly coloured and tender. Transfer to a dish with a slotted spoon, cover and keep hot.

3   Add the onion and peppers to the pan and sprinkle with the salt. Cook gently, stirring occasionally, for 10 minutes until soft. Meanwhile, boil the stock until reduced by half, stirring in the warm sesame oil and peanut butter when the stock is simmering well.

To Serve Slice the chicken on the diagonal and arrange on warm plates. Spoon the sauce over the chicken and the pepper mixture alongside. Serve immediately.

Chef's Tip

You can buy small bottles of both green and red Thai curry paste in supermarkets, and sachets or packets of freshly made paste in the chilled sections of oriental shops and some gourmet delicatessens. Alternatively, you can make your own using the recipe on page 186.

CHICKEN WITH MUSHROOMS AND LEEKS

CHICKEN BREASTS ARE made succulent with a stuffing of leeks and a mushroom and sherry sauce. Serve with mangetouts and boiled new potatoes tossed in butter and chopped fresh herbs.

Serves 4

Preparation time: 30 mnutes

Cooking time:
20-25 minutes

2 leeks (white part only), weighing about 175 g (6 oz)
250 g (8 oz) white button mushrooms
1 garlic clove
125 g (4 oz) butter
salt and freshly ground black pepper
125 ml (4 fl oz) sunflower oil
200 ml (7 fl oz) hot chicken stock
4 skinless boneless chicken breasts, each weighing 175–200 g (6–7 oz)
4 tablespoons sherry

Chef's Tips

This is an excellent dish for entertaining because the chicken breasts can be prepared and stuffed the day before. Cover them with cling film and keep them in the refrigerator. Make the mushroom sauce and cook the chicken immediately before serving.

If there are too many leeks to fit inside the pockets in the chicken, mix any left over into the mushrooms.

1   Cut the leeks into very thin strips, then wash them well in cold water. Leave to soak in fresh cold water for 2 minutes. Slice the mushrooms. Crush the garlic.

2   Melt half the butter in a sauté pan over low heat. Drain the leeks and add them to the hot butter. Cover the pan and cook over low heat until the leeks are soft, about 5 minutes. Transfer to a bowl, season and allow to cool.

3   Heat half the oil in the sauté pan, add the mushrooms, garlic and salt and pepper and sauté over high heat. Drain off any excess liquid, add the stock and leave to simmer until reduced by about half. Remove from the heat.

4   Carefully cut open each chicken breast lengthways to make a pocket in the centre. Fill the pockets with the leeks. Season the chicken. Melt the remaining butter and oil in a frying pan, add the chicken and brown over moderate heat. After about 3 minutes, turn the chicken over and reduce the heat slightly. Cook for a further 5-7 minutes, basting frequently. Transfer the chicken breasts to warm plates, cover and keep hot.

To Serve   Deglaze the pan with the sherry, then mix this into the mushrooms and heat through until bubbling and thickened. Taste for seasoning, spoon over and around the chicken and serve immediately.

CHICKEN AND CASHEWS

Serves 2-3

Preparation time: 15 minutes

Cooking time:
about 10 minutes

Chef's Tip

Coating the chicken in egg white and cornflour is a Chinese technique that helps protect the delicate fibres of the meat from the high heat used in stir-frying. It may take a little extra time, but it is well worth it because it ensures a tender, moist result.

THE DARK, ALMOST black chillies make a dramatic colour contrast against the whiteness of the chicken in this Chinese stir-fry. Serve it very simply, with boiled egg or buckwheat noodles.

500 g (1 lb) skinless boneless
   chicken breasts
4-5 cm (1½–2 inch) piece of fresh
   root ginger
½ teaspoon salt
¼ teaspoon freshly ground black pepper
1 teaspoon rice wine or sherry
1 teaspoon sesame oil
2 large egg whites
2 teaspoons cornflour
4 spring onions
4 tablespoons groundnut oil
5 dried chillies
60–90 g (2–3 oz) cashew nuts

Sauce
2 teaspoons cornflour
2 teaspoons rice wine or sherry
2 tablespoons soy sauce
1 teaspoon white vinegar
1–2 tablespoons sugar, to taste
2 teaspoons sesame oil
300 ml (½ pint) chicken stock

1   Cut the chicken into bite-sized pieces and place in a bowl. Grate about one-third of the ginger over the chicken, then add the salt, pepper, rice wine or sherry and sesame oil. Lightly beat the egg whites and mix into the chicken with the cornflour. Cover and set aside while preparing the remaining ingredients.

2   Shred the remaining ginger. Cut the spring onions into 5 cm (2 inch) lengths. Prepare the sauce. In a small bowl, mix the cornflour with 1 tablespoon cold water, then add the remaining sauce ingredients and mix until smooth.

3   Heat the oil in a wok or deep sauté pan over moderate heat. Add the chillies and stir-fry until they begin to darken in colour. Increase the heat to high and continue stirring until the chillies are almost black.

4   Add the chicken and stir-fry until it is white, then add the ginger, spring onions, cashews and the sauce mixture. Stir-fry until all the ingredients are glossy and the sauce has thickened, 3-4 minutes.

To Serve Turn into a warm serving bowl and serve immediately.

CHICKEN WITH GOAT'S CHEESE EN PAPILLOTE

Serves 4

Preparation time: 20 minutes

Cooking time: 25 minutes

Chef's Tips

Any type of goat's cheese can be used for the stuffing. If you buy one of the hard kinds, leave it to soften at room temperature before using. This will make it easier to push into the chicken pockets.

If you like, you can wrap each chicken breast in a slice of prosciutto (Parma ham) before sitting it on the vegetables. This will make the chicken more moist.

The chicken will keep hot en papillote for 15-20 minutes, so you can remove it from the oven and let it sit unopened while you are eating the first course.

RESH AND LIGHT, this main course has a Mediterranean flavour, just perfect for an al fresco summer lunch. The papillotes can be prepared the day before, so all you have to do is pop them in the oven half an hour before serving.

4 large skinless boneless chicken breasts
90 g (3 oz) goat's cheese
salt and freshly ground black pepper
1 large head of fennel
2 medium to large ripe tomatoes
12 black olives
1 tablespoon olive oil
4 tablespoons dry white wine or vermouth

1   Preheat the oven to 200°C (400°F) Gas 6. With a sharp pointed knife, make an incision in the rounded side and down the length of each chicken breast, cutting not quite to the ends. Gently open the breast and move the knife to left and right to make a pocket. Divide the cheese into quarters. Using your fingers, stuff one-quarter of the cheese into each chicken pocket. Season with pepper, then close the chicken to conceal the cheese.

2   Trim and finely slice the fennel, saving the feathery tops for the garnish. Peel and slice the tomatoes. Stone and roughly chop the olives. Heat the oil in a pan, add the fennel and sauté for about 5 minutes until softened and lightly coloured.

3   Lightly oil 4 large circles or squares of foil, baking parchment or greaseproof paper. Place the fennel in the middle of each, scatter with the olives and arrange the tomato slices on top. Season. Place the stuffed chicken breasts on top of the tomatoes and spoon 1 tablespoon wine or vermouth over each. Close the parcels and seal tightly to make papillotes. Place in a baking dish and bake for 25 minutes.

To Serve Open the papillotes, taking care to avoid the escaping hot steam. With a fish slice, carefully transfer the chicken and vegetables to warm plates. Arrange a few fennel slices on top of each breast and spoon over any juices. Garnish with the reserved fennel tops and serve immediately.

CHICKEN JALFREZI

THIS IS A fresh and buttery medium-hot curry from India, where the name 'jalfrezi' is used to describe a sauté or stir-fry. Serve it with mango chutney and lime pickle, and a simple Rice Pilaf (page 140).

500 g (1 lb) skinless boneless chicken breasts

1 medium onion

1 garlic clove

1 small handful of fresh coriander leaves

2.5 cm (1 inch) piece of fresh root ginger

60 g (2 oz) butter

2 tablespoons sunflower oil

1 teaspoon turmeric

1 teaspoon chilli powder

½ teaspoon salt

1 x 400 g can chopped tomatoes

1 teaspoon ground cumin

1 teaspoon ground coriander

1 teaspoon garam masala

Serves 4

Preparation time: 15 minutes

Cooking time:
about 25 minutes

Variation

You can use 4 large fresh tomatoes instead of canned tomatoes. Make sure they are ripe and juicy and peel them before chopping them finely. To peel tomatoes quickly, cut a cross in the rounded end of each tomato, put the tomatoes in a bowl and pour boiling water over them. Lift them out one at a time and immerse in a bowl of cold water – the skins should then peel off easily.

1   Cut the chicken into strips or cubes. Finely slice the onion. Chop the garlic and fresh coriander, keeping them separate. Peel and grate the ginger.

2   Melt half the butter with the oil in a large sauté pan, add the onion and stir over low heat for a few minutes until softened. Add the chicken, garlic, turmeric, chilli powder and salt. Increase the heat to moderate and fry for 5 minutes. Stir and scrape the bottom of the pan constantly to ensure the spices do not burn.

3   Add the tomatoes, stir to combine, then cover and simmer for 15 minutes, stirring occasionally. Add the remaining butter, the ground spices, fresh ginger and half the fresh coriander. Stir and simmer for a few minutes until the fat shimmers around the edge of the sauce.

To Serve   Taste and add more salt if necessary, turn into a warm serving bowl and sprinkle with the remaining fresh coriander. Serve hot.

COQ AU VIN

THIS IS AN easy version of the classic bistro recipe that everyone loves. Serve it in true French style with new potatoes tossed in butter and finely chopped flat-leaf parsley, then follow with a green salad dressed with Vinaigrette (page 188).

Serves 4

Preparation time: 30 minutes

Cooking time: about 1 hour

1 small onion
1 small carrot
1 small celery stick
20 pickling onions
salt and freshly ground black pepper
8 chicken pieces
2 tablespoons sunflower oil
90 g (3 oz) lardons or thickly diced bacon
20 whole button mushrooms
500 ml (16 fl oz) red wine, preferably Burgundy
400 ml (14 fl oz) hot chicken stock
1 bouquet garni
finely chopped fresh flat-leaf parsley, to garnish

Chef's Tips

You can either buy a whole chicken and joint it yourself, or buy ready cut pieces from the supermarket. Legs, thighs and wings are a good choice, all with bone in. It is a matter of personal taste whether you leave the skin on or not.

Pickling onions can be fiddly to peel. If you blanch them first you will find the task easier. Put them in a pan, cover with cold water and bring to the boil. Boil for 2-3 minutes, then drain and rinse under cold running water.

1   Finely chop the onion, carrot and celery. Peel the pickling onions (see Chef's Tips). Season the chicken. Heat the oil in a flameproof casserole, add the chicken and brown in the hot oil. Remove and set aside. Add the lardons or bacon and cook for 2-3 minutes, then add the mushrooms and toss until lightly coloured. With a slotted spoon, remove the lardons or bacon and mushrooms and set aside.

2   Add the chopped vegetables to the pan and cook, stirring, for a few minutes. Add the wine and reduce by about half, then add the stock, whole pickling onions and bouquet garni. Bring to the boil. Return the chicken to the pan, cover and simmer gently for 30-40 minutes until tender.

3   Remove the chicken and pickling onions and keep hot. Discard the bouquet garni. Boil the liquid until reduced and slightly thickened, then add the lardons and mushrooms and stir until hot.

To Serve Taste the sauce for seasoning, return the chicken and onions to the pan and sprinkle with chopped parsley. Serve hot.

DUCK BREASTS WITH HONEY CORIANDER SAUCE

A MAIN COURSE FOR a special dinner à deux. Its delicate oriental flavour is best complemented with a simple dish of stir-fried egg noodles and vegetables. Spring onions and red pepper are a good choice.

1 large duck breast (magret), weighing at least 250 g (8 oz)
salt and freshly ground black pepper
2 tablespoons coriander seeds
125 ml (4 fl oz) runny honey
4 tablespoons soy sauce
175 ml (6 fl oz) hot chicken stock
fresh coriander sprigs, to garnish

Serves 2

Preparation time: 10 minutes

Cooking time:
about 30 minutes

Chef's Tip

Magrets, boneless duck breasts, originally only came from Barbary ducks, but this is not always the case these days. You will find them at large supermarkets and specialist butchers. The ones imported from France are usually sold in vacuum packs. They are rich and meaty, and in France it is the custom to serve 1 large magret between 2 people, but check the weight when buying – you may need to serve 1 duck breast for each person.

1   Trim off any excess fat and skin from the duck to neaten its appearance, then score the fat in a criss-cross pattern and season both sides with salt and pepper.

2   Dry-fry the coriander seeds in a non-stick frying pan until they give off a spicy aroma and are dark in colour, then put them in a mortar and crush with a pestle. Put the honey and soy sauce in a small saucepan and slowly bring to the boil, stirring. Add the stock and crushed coriander seeds and cook at a low boil until reduced, about 10 minutes. Remove from the heat.

3   Put the duck breast, fat-side down, in a frying pan and place over moderate heat. Cook for 10 minutes, pressing the duck frequently with a fish slice to keep it as flat as possible. Pour off the excess fat from the pan, turn the duck over and cook for a further 7 minutes or until done to your liking. Meanwhile, strain the sauce through a sieve into a clean pan and reheat gently.

To Serve Carve the duck on the diagonal into very thin slices and arrange in a fan shape on warm dinner plates. Drizzle the sauce over the slices, garnish each portion with a dainty sprig of coriander and serve immediately.

Beef Carbonnade

TRADITIONAL AND HEARTY Flemish casserole for a cold winter's evening. Serve with jacket baked potatoes topped with butter and soured cream, and a fresh green vegetable such as broccoli.

Serves 4-6

Preparation time: 5 minutes

Cooking time: 1½-2 hours

1 large onion
3 tablespoons sunflower oil
1 kg (2 lb) braising steak, cut into thick slices
30 g (1 oz) plain flour
1 x 275 ml can sweet stout
about 750 ml (1¼ pints) hot beef stock
1 bouquet garni
2 juniper berries
1 tablespoon Dijon mustard
2 teaspoons soft brown sugar
salt and freshly ground black pepper

Chef's Tip

It is traditional to use sliced meat for a carbonnade, but you can cut it into squares if you prefer. Keep them quite large – about 5 cm (2 inches) – or they will cook too quickly and become dry.

1   Preheat the oven to 180°C (350°F) Gas 4. Thinly slice the onion. In a large flame-proof casserole, heat the oil over moderately high heat and brown the sliced beef in batches until nicely coloured on both sides. Once browned, remove and set aside.

2   Lower the heat and cook the onion for 3-5 minutes until lightly coloured, then add the flour. Stir well for 1 minute. Add the stout and allow to simmer for 5 minutes, stirring well. Add the remaining ingredients, season to taste and bring to the boil.

3   Cover the casserole and put it in the oven. Cook for 1¼-1¾ hours or until the meat is tender. Check the level of the cooking liquid from time to time and add more stock if necessary.

To Serve   Discard the bouquet garni and taste the sauce for seasoning. Arrange the slices of meat on warm plates and spoon the sauce over them. Serve hot.

BEEF POT ROAST WITH RED WINE

THE PERFECT DISH FOR a weekend lunch – all the preparation can be done the day before, then the meat can be slowly simmered in the oven during the morning. Serve with Mashed Potatoes (page 135) and a seasonal vegetable or two.

1 large carrot	1 tablespoon plain flour
1 small onion	2 tablespoons tomato purée
1 medium celery stick	1 bouquet garni
2 garlic cloves	salt and freshly ground black pepper
2–3 tablespoons sunflower oil	400 ml (14 fl oz) red wine
1.5 kg (3 lb) rolled and tied top rump of beef	600 ml (1 pint) hot beef stock

Serves 4-6

Preparation time: 20 minutes

Cooking time: 2½-3 hours

1 Preheat the oven to 170°C (325°F) Gas 3. Finely chop all the vegetables and the garlic, keeping them separate. Heat the oil in a large flameproof casserole and sear the meat over moderately high heat until browned on all sides. Remove and set aside.

2 Pour off any excess fat from the pan and reduce the heat to medium-low. Add the carrot, onion and celery and sauté for 2-3 minutes. Add the flour and tomato purée, stir well and cook for 1 minute, then add the wine, garlic, bouquet garni and salt and pepper to taste.

3 Return the meat to the casserole and simmer until the wine has reduced by about one-third. Add the stock and return to a simmer, then cover the casserole and put it in the oven. Cook for 2-2½ hours or until the meat is very tender.

4 Remove the meat and keep hot. Strain the cooking liquid through a fine sieve, return to the casserole and simmer until reduced to your liking. Taste for seasoning.

To Serve Slice the meat and place on a warm platter. Spoon some of the sauce over the meat and serve immediately, with the remaining sauce handed separately in a sauce boat.

Chef's Tips

Top rump is a good joint for pot roasting. You may not be able to find it ready rolled and tied at the supermarket, but any butcher will do this for you. Less expensive topside, brisket and silverside are often sold ready rolled and tied. They can be used, but you may not get such succulent results.

Beef joints are often sold with fat tied around them. This helps keep them moist, but you may need to skim and blot the sauce with kitchen paper after straining.

BEEF STROGANOFF

A GOOD DISH FOR an evening at home when you want to serve something special but haven't much time to spend in the kitchen. Serve with rice and a salad of mixed leaves tossed with Vinaigrette (page 188).

250 g (8 oz) beef fillet (tail end) or good-quality rump or sirloin steak
1 large shallot or 1 small onion
1 small garlic clove
30 g (1 oz) butter
1 rounded teaspoon paprika
2 tablespoons sunflower oil
salt and freshly ground black pepper

Serves 2

Preparation time:
10-15 minutes

Cooking time:
about 10 minutes

To Serve

150 ml (¼ pint) crème fraîche
1 dill or sweet and sour cucumber, cut into julienne
1–2 tablespoons finely chopped fresh flat-leaf parsley

Chef's Tip

Be sure to fry the beef over high heat. If the heat is too low, the juices will run out of the meat and result in a stewed appearance and taste.

Variation

If you have some brandy to hand, add 1 tablespoon to the cooked shallot or onion and reduce it down to nothing before adding the garlic and paprika.

1   Trim the meat of any fat and sinew, then cut it into strips about 4 cm (1½ inches) long and 5 mm (¼ inch) thick. Finely chop the shallot or onion. Crush the garlic.

2   Melt the butter in a frying pan, add the shallot or onion and cook over low heat for 5-7 minutes until soft and translucent. Stir in the garlic and paprika. Cook for 1 minute, stirring. Remove the mixture from the pan and set aside.

3   Add the oil to the pan and heat it over high heat. When it sizzles, add the beef and toss for 2-3 minutes until the beef is sealed and lightly browned. Stir in the shallot mixture and salt and pepper to taste and heat through, stirring.

To Serve Swirl in the crème fraîche and serve immediately, topped with the cucumber julienne and the parsley.

SALTIMBOCCA

LITERALLY TRANSLATED, SALTIMBOCCA means 'jump in the mouth', and these bite-sized nuggets of veal wrapped around sage and prosciutto seem delicious enough to do just that. Serve them Italian style, with courgettes, broccoli or beans.

4 thin slices of veal escalope, each weighing about 150 g (5 oz)
black pepper
1 small bunch of fresh sage
100 g (3½ oz) prosciutto (Parma ham)
3–4 tablespoons olive oil
250 ml (8 fl oz) dry white wine
salt
fresh sage sprigs, to garnish

Serves 4

Preparation time:
about 30 minutes

Cooking time:
about 10 minutes

1   Put the veal between cling film and pound with the base of a saucepan until thin. Cut each escalope into small squares or rectangles, making about 30 pieces in all.

2   Grind pepper over the veal, then place 1-2 small sage leaves on top of each piece. Cut the prosciutto into small pieces and arrange over the sage. Roll up each piece of veal and secure with a wooden toothpick.

3   Heat the oil in a large frying pan over moderate to high heat. Add the saltimbocca in batches and cook for no longer than 2-3 minutes, until browned on all sides. Remove and keep hot. Add the wine to the pan and boil until reduced, stirring to loosen any browned bits from the bottom of the pan. Season to taste.

To Serve Remove the toothpicks from the saltimbocca and arrange the veal on a warm serving platter. Pour the sauce over, garnish with fresh sage sprigs and serve immediately.

Chef's Tips

Although the preparation of the veal rolls may seem long, the cooking time compensates in that it is very short. The rolls can be prepared up to 24 hours in advance and kept, covered, in the refrigerator.

Veal escalope is a delicate and naturally tender meat. Do not overcook it or it will be dry and tough.

LAMB COUSCOUS

Serves 4-6

Preparation time:
15-20 minutes

Cooking time:
about 1¼ hours

Chef's Tip

Harissa is a fiery, thick sauce made from chillies, garlic and spices. It is sold in tubes, cans and jars at most supermarkets. The tubes are the most convenient to use. Add it sparingly at first, until you get the degree of heat you like, and serve more in a little bowl at the table for those who like their food extra hot.

A TUNISIAN STEW WITH a wonderful aroma and flavour. A meal in itself that needs no accompaniment, it is ideal for informal entertaining. The meat and vegetables taste better when cooked the day before.

1 kg (2 lb) boneless lamb shoulder or neck fillet	2 tablespoons tomato purée
2 medium red onions	1 bouquet garni
8–12 baby new potatoes	1 teaspoon sea salt
4 carrots	1 turnip, weighing about 200 g (7 oz)
2 tomatoes, total weight about 150 g (5 oz)	2 courgettes
2 garlic cloves	1 x 400 g can chickpeas
3 tablespoons olive oil	250 g (8 oz) quick-cooking couscous
1 teaspoon turmeric	½–1 teaspoon harissa, or to taste
	chopped fresh coriander, to garnish

1   Trim the lamb of any excess fat, then cut the meat into small pieces. Quarter the onions. Halve or quarter the potatoes (there is no need to peel them). Peel the carrots and cut them into large pieces. Chop the tomatoes and crush the garlic.

2   Heat the oil in a large pan and brown the lamb in batches over high heat. Return all of the lamb to the pan and add the onions, potatoes, carrots and turmeric. Stir well, add the tomato purée and stir again. Add the tomatoes and garlic and enough cold water to cover, then add the bouquet garni and salt and bring to a simmer. Cover and cook for 30 minutes.

3   Peel and quarter the turnip. Cut the courgettes into large pieces. Drain and rinse the chickpeas. Add the turnip, courgettes and chickpeas to the pan and cook for 30 minutes or until the lamb is tender. Meanwhile, cook the couscous according to the instructions on the packet.

To Serve Remove the bouquet garni from the stew, then stir in harissa to taste. Pile the couscous in warm dishes or bowls and spoon the stew on top. Sprinkle with fresh coriander and serve.

LAMB KEBABS WITH TOMATO AND CORIANDER SALSA

TANGY HOT KEBABS taste sensational with a cool and refreshing salsa. This is a good recipe for a barbecue party because everything can be prepared the day before and the lamb cooked at the last minute. Saffron rice makes a colourful accompaniment.

4 large ripe tomatoes
1 handful of fresh coriander
1 small red onion
juice of 1½ lemons
5 tablespoons olive oil
salt and freshly ground black pepper
2 garlic cloves
750 g (1½ lb) boneless lamb shoulder, leg or neck fillet,
    cut into 2 cm (¾ inch) cubes

Serves 4

Preparation time: about 20 minutes, plus marinating

Cooking time: 8-12 minutes

1   Dice the tomatoes and remove the seeds, then place in a bowl. Finely chop the coriander and onion. Put one-third of the coriander and onion in the bowl with the tomatoes, add one-third of the lemon juice, 2 tablespoons of the olive oil and salt and pepper to taste. Toss the salsa well to mix, cover with cling film and refrigerate while preparing and marinating the lamb.

2   Chop the garlic and place in a large bowl with the lamb. Add the remaining coriander, onion, lemon juice and oil. Season with salt and pepper. Toss until the lamb is well coated, cover with cling film and leave to marinate in the refrigerator for at least 4 hours, preferably overnight.

3   Thread the lamb on skewers and cook on the barbecue or under a preheated very hot grill for 8-10 minutes, turning the skewers as necessary.

To Serve   Arrange the skewers of lamb on a bed of saffron rice, with the chilled salsa alongside.

Variations

Use chicken instead of lamb, either breast meat or boneless thighs.

Marinate the meat in Spiced Yogurt Marinade (page 186) instead of the marinade given here, and serve with Rice Pilaf (page 140) and Cucumber and Mint Raita (page 152).

LAMB WITH PEPPERS AND TOMATO

A colourful sauté simply oozing with flavour, good in late summer or early autumn when peppers are at their best. Serve with a plain accompaniment, such as Mashed Potatoes (page 135), boiled polenta or rice.

1 kg (2 lb) boneless lamb shoulder or neck fillet
salt and freshly ground black pepper
3 small peppers (red, yellow and green)
1 onion
4 garlic cloves
3 tablespoons olive oil
½ x 400 g can chopped tomatoes
1 tablespoon sun-dried tomato paste
200 ml (7 fl oz) dry white wine
1 bouquet garni
100 g (3½ oz) prosciutto di Parma (Parma ham) or other cured ham
1 tablespoon chopped fresh flat-leaf parsley
fresh flat-leaf parsley sprigs, to garnish

Serves 4

Preparation time: 20 minutes

**Cooking time:
about 55 minutes**

Chef's Tips

For speed, buy the lamb from the butcher and ask him to cut it into squares for you, trimming off as much fat as possible. At the supermarket, boneless shoulder of lamb is often sold rolled and tied as a joint, but it doesn't take many minutes to undo it and cut it into squares. Neck fillet is usually sold in the piece, rather like pork fillet or tenderloin.

The prosciutto for serving is a professional chef's touch, but it can be omitted.

1   Trim the lamb of any excess fat, then cut the meat into 2.5 cm (1 inch) squares and season with salt and pepper. Slice the the peppers and onion. Chop the garlic.

2   Heat 2 tablespoons of the oil in a large flameproof casserole and brown the lamb in batches over high heat. Remove with a slotted spoon and set aside. Reduce the heat to low and add the peppers and onion. Cook gently until softened, stirring and scraping the sediment from the bottom of the pan.

3   Add the garlic, tomatoes and tomato paste, then return the lamb to the casserole and add the wine and bouquet garni. Bring to the boil, cover and lower the heat to a gentle simmer. Cook for 45 minutes or until the lamb is tender, stirring occasionally. At the end of cooking, discard the bouquet garni and taste the lamb for seasoning.

To Serve Quickly sear the prosciutto in the remaining oil. Place in the bottom of a warm serving dish and spoon the lamb on top. Sprinkle with the chopped parsley and serve immediately, garnished with parsley sprigs.

ROAST LAMB WITH GARLIC AND THYME

A SIMPLE JOINT FOR Sunday lunch, with a superbly flavoured gravy made French chef style. Serve with Roasted Mediterranean Vegetables (page 128) and Mashed Potatoes (page 135) mixed with chopped fresh herbs.

6 garlic cloves
1 small carrot
1 small onion
1 small celery stick
1 boned and rolled joint of lamb (leg or shoulder), weighing about 1.8 kg (3½ lb)
salt and freshly ground black pepper
90 g (3 oz) butter, softened
300 ml (½ pint) dry white wine
500 ml (16 fl oz) hot lamb or beef stock
1 fresh thyme sprig
1 bay leaf

Serves 6

Preparation time: 15 minutes

Cooking time:
about 1¼ hours

Chef's Tips

If buying the lamb from a butcher, ask him for the bones from the joint and get him to chop them into small pieces. You can then add them to the roasting tin with the chopped vegetables to make a richer gravy.

The cooking time given here is short, because roast lamb is generally served rare in France. If you prefer it medium, cook for another 10-15 minutes.

1 Preheat the oven to 190°C (375°F) Gas 5. Cut the garlic cloves in half. Roughly chop the carrot, onion and celery. Rub the lamb all over with the cut side of 2 of the garlic clove halves, then rub all over with salt and pepper. Place the lamb in a roasting tin and spread with the butter.

2 Roast the lamb for 30 minutes, then turn the joint over and spread the chopped vegetables and remaining garlic around. Roast for another 30 minutes, or until done to your liking. Remove the lamb, cover with tented foil and keep hot. Turn the oven down to 110°C (225°F) Gas ¼.

3 Tip the contents of the roasting tin into a large sieve and let the fat strain through into a bowl. Discard the fat. Return the vegetables to the roasting tin and place on the hob. Deglaze with the wine, scraping the tin to dissolve the sediment, then simmer, stirring, until the wine has almost evaporated.

4 Add the stock, thyme sprig and bay leaf to the tin. Bring to the boil, stirring, then simmer until reduced by about two-thirds. Meanwhile, carve the lamb, arrange the slices on a warm platter and cover with foil. Reheat in the oven for 3-5 minutes.

To Serve Strain the sauce into a sauce boat and serve with the platter of lamb.

PORK MEDALLIONS WITH LEEKS AND MUSTARD SAUCE

Serves 4

Preparation time: 20 minutes

Cooking time:
·20-25 minutes

A MINGLING OF FRENCH and oriental flavours makes this a very special dish. It goes well with Gratin Dauphinois (page 139), which is baked in the oven, leaving you free to concentrate on cooking the pork on top of the stove.

750 g (1½ lb) pork fillet (tenderloin)
3 garlic cloves
3 tablespoons soy sauce
2 tablespoons rice wine or sherry
a good pinch of sugar
625 g (1¼ lb) small leeks
30 g (1 oz) butter
2–3 tablespoons dry white wine
2 tablespoons sunflower oil
fresh sage leaves, to garnish

Mustard Sauce
3 shallots
1 tablespoon sunflower oil
30 g (1 oz) sugar
3 tablespoons white wine vinegar
4 tablespoons dry vermouth
200 ml (7 fl oz) canned beef
  consommé
1 tablespoon wholegrain mustard
salt and freshly ground black pepper

Chef's Tips

The pork and leeks require last-minute cooking, so have all the ingredients prepared and assembled before you start.

You can buy washed and sliced leeks in bags at many supermarkets. They are a little more expensive than whole leeks, but save a lot of time and trouble.

The pork can be sliced and put in the marinade the day before, then left to marinate in the refrigerator overnight. The sauce can also be made and strained the day before, but do not add the mustard at this stage. While the pork is cooking, gently reheat the sauce, then add the mustard.

1   Trim the pork and reserve the trimmings for the sauce. Cut the pork into slices on the diagonal about 2.5 cm (1 inch) thick. Finely chop the garlic and mix it in a large bowl with the soy sauce, rice wine or sherry and the sugar. Put the pork in the bowl, stir to coat in the marinade, then set aside. Trim the leeks and cut them on the diagonal into thick slices.

2   Make the mustard sauce. Finely chop the shallots and reserved pork trimmings. Fry them in the oil with the sugar until lightly caramelized. Deglaze the pan with the vinegar, then reduce until syrupy. Add the vermouth and reduce until syrupy. Pour in the consommé and cook for 10-15 minutes. Strain into a clean pan, then add the mustard and seasoning. Cover and keep hot.

3   Melt the butter in a sauté pan and add the leeks, wine and salt and pepper to taste. Cover the pan with a lid and gently steam the leeks. At the same time, heat the oil in a separate sauté pan and sauté the pork slices over moderate to high heat for 3-4 minutes on each side.

To Serve   Arrange a bed of leeks on each warm plate and place the pork on top. Drizzle the sauce over the pork and garnish with sage leaves. Serve immediately.

PORK FILLETS ZINGARA

R ICH AND EARTHY TASTING, this is a rustic dish which makes a good main course for an autumn or winter dinner party. Serve it with Mashed Potatoes (page 135) or Polenta (page 136), and follow with a tossed green salad.

750 g (1½ lb) pork fillet (tenderloin)
1 tablespoon paprika
salt and freshly ground black pepper
2 medium to large tomatoes
2 shallots
60 g (2 oz) mushrooms
60 g (2 oz) cooked ham
60 g (2 oz) cooked tongue
30 g (1 oz) butter
2 tablespoons olive oil
4 tablespoons Madeira
300 ml (½ pint) hot chicken stock
finely chopped fresh parsley, to garnish

Serves 4

Preparation time:
20 minutes

Cooking time:
about 15 minutes

1   Trim the pork and reserve the trimmings for the sauce. Cut the pork into slices on the diagonal about 2.5 cm (1 inch) thick. Mix the paprika on a plate with salt and pepper to taste, then use to coat the pork. Peel, deseed and finely chop the tomatoes. Finely chop the shallots. Shred the mushrooms, ham and tongue.

2   Melt the butter with 1 tablespoon of the oil in a sauté pan and sauté the pork over moderate to high heat for 3-4 minutes on each side. Remove the pork from the pan with tongs or a slotted spoon and keep hot.

3   Lower the heat under the pan, add the shallots and reserved pork trimmings and stir for 1 minute before adding the Madeira. Increase the heat to moderate and cook until almost dry, then add the tomatoes and stock. Lower the heat and simmer until thickened. Meanwhile, sauté the mushrooms in the remaining oil in a separate pan.

4   Stir the mushrooms, ham and tongue into the sauce, season to taste and heat through.

To Serve   Place the pork on warm plates and coat with the sauce. Sprinkle with parsley and serve immediately.

Chef's Tip

Zingara means 'gypsy style' in classic French cuisine, and it is used to describe a dish flavoured with ham, tongue, mushrooms and sometimes truffles. The sauce is traditionally based on Madeira, but if you don't have any, you can use port or red wine instead.

PORK WITH PESTO

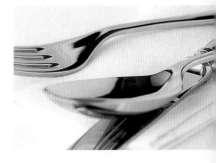

An IDEAL DISH for last-minute entertaining because it is so quick and easy to prepare and cook. Serve with a julienne of courgettes, leeks and carrots or orange pepper. Boiled polenta is another suitable accompaniment.

1 whole pork fillet (tenderloin), weighing about 375 g (12 oz)
1 heaped tablespoon plain flour
salt and freshly ground black pepper
2 tablespoons olive oil
about 3 tablespoons bottled or homemade Basil Pesto (page 185)
125 ml (4 fl oz) medium sherry or Vouvray white wine
fresh basil leaves, to garnish

Serves 2-3

Preparation time: 10 minutes

Cooking time:
about 8 minutes

1 Trim the pork fillet, then cut the meat on the diagonal into 2.5 cm (1 inch) slices; you should get about 10 slices. Place the slices on a board and flatten them with the base of a saucepan or a meat mallet until about 1.25 cm (½ inch) thick.

2 Preheat the grill. Spread the flour out on a plate and season well. Put the pork slices on the flour and turn to coat. Heat the oil in a large frying pan and fry the pork slices for 2 minutes on each side.

3 Transfer the slices of pork to the rack of the grill pan. Set the frying pan aside. Spread the top of each pork slice with pesto and grill for 30-60 seconds until bubbling. Transfer to warm plates and keep hot.

4 Add the sherry or wine to the frying pan and stir over moderate heat until well mixed with any sediment and meat juices in the pan. Pour over the pork.

To Serve Garnish with fresh basil and serve immediately.

Chef's Tips

The meat can be sliced and coated in seasoned flour up to 24 hours in advance, then covered and kept in the refrigerator.

Watch the pork closely under the grill and do not grill the pesto for longer than 30-60 seconds or it may burn.

SAUSAGE AND MASH WITH ONION GRAVY

Serves 4

Preparation time: 15 minutes

Cooking time:
about 35 minutes

Chef's Tip

Start boiling the potatoes for the mash before frying the sausages, then while the sausages are cooking you will have your hands free to mash the potatoes. You can then reheat the potatoes, adding the hot milk and butter, just before the onion gravy is ready.

A N OLD-FASHIONED favourite that is always popular, especially on cold winter evenings. This version is rather special, so buy good-quality, pure pork sausages from your butcher or supermarket.

8 large sausages
1 large Spanish onion
2 tablespoons sunflower oil
60 g (2 oz) butter
1 tablespoon plain flour
500 ml (16 fl oz) hot beef stock
salt and freshly ground black pepper
Mashed Potatoes (page 135)
fresh sage sprigs, to garnish

1 Prick the sausages. Thinly slice the onion into rings. Heat the oil in a large frying pan, add the sausages and fry gently for about 15 minutes until cooked through and browned on all sides. Remove and keep hot.

2 Add the butter to the pan and heat gently until melted. Add the onion rings and cook over low heat for 3-5 minutes, stirring constantly, then lightly colour them over high heat for 2-3 minutes.

3 Sprinkle in the flour, lower the heat and cook, stirring, for 1-2 minutes. Pour in the hot stock and bring to the boil, stirring. Lower the heat, add salt and pepper to taste and simmer for about 10 minutes.

To Serve Mound the mashed potatoes on warm plates and arrange the sausages on top. Spoon the gravy over and around and serve immediately, garnished with fresh sage.

Weekend Entertaining
menu ideas

CELEBRATION DINNER PARTY
—

Smoked Duck with Broccoli and Almonds

•

Seafood Fricassee
Boiled New Potatoes
Mangetouts with Herbs

•

Lemon Tart

✑

SUNDAY ROAST LUNCH
—

Courgette and Roasted Garlic Soup

•

Roast Lamb with Garlic and Thyme
Normandy Carrots
Green Beans with Leeks and Tomatoes
Mashed Potatoes

•

Plum and Cinnamon Crumble

✑

THAI LUNCH OR DINNER
—

Prawn and Ginger Soup

•

Thai Chicken with Peppers
Jasmine Rice

•

Fragrant Fruit Salad

✑

SUMMER LUNCH PARTY
—

Layered Vegetable Terrine

•

Scallops with Tomato and Saffron
Boiled Rice
Leafy Mixed Salad

•

Raspberry Fool

✑

WINTER DINNER PARTY
—

Warm Scallop Salad

•

Duck Breasts with Honey Coriander Sauce
Spinach with Coriander and Cream
Gratin Dauphinois

•

Chocolate Vacherin

✑

SEAFOOD DINNER PARTY

—

Grilled Mussels with Lime and Pesto

•

Sole with Smoked Salmon
New Potatoes with Butter and Herbs

•

Ginger Crème Brûlée

⌒

A CHINESE MEAL

—

Asparagus with Soy and Wasabi Dressing

•

Chicken and Cashews

Egg Noodles

•

Fragrant Fruit Salad

⌒

AL FRESCO SUMMER LUNCH

—

Cucumber and Dill Soup

•

Fish Kebabs with Lime and Rosemary
Boiled Rice

•

Eton Mess

⌒

SATURDAY SUPPER PARTY

—

Warm Potato Salad

•

Salmon with Rosemary Cream
Roasted Mediterranean Vegetables

•

White Chocolate and Cream Cheese Tart

⌒

INDIAN CURRY LUNCH

—

Chicken Jalfrezi
Rice Pilaf
Cucumber and Mint Raita

•

Cardamom Crème Brûlée

⌒

FRENCH BISTRO SUPPER

—

Seared Scallops with Roasted Pepper Coulis

•

Coq au Vin
Gratin Dauphinois
Green Salad

•

Crêpes Suzette

⌒

ITALIAN SUPPER PARTY

—

Fresh Tomato and Pepper Soup with Basil

•

Risotto with Peas and Prosciutto

•

Saltimbocca

•

Roasted Fruit with Mascarpone Cream

⌒

DINNER À DEUX

—

Avocado with Grapefruit and Vinaigrette

•

Steak with Green Peppercorn Sauce

•

Chocolate and Pecan Yogurt Ice-Cream

⌒

Vegetables, Salads & Accompaniments

Fresh seasonal vegetables are an absolute boon for the busy cook because they taste best when cooked as quickly and simply as possible, and they also retain more of their vitamins and minerals this way. The quick and easy ideas on pages 154-155 give you all the basic information you need to cook and serve most of the popular vegetables, while the recipes in this chapter go one step further to bring you some of Le Cordon Bleu's international side dishes.

If you are in a hurry, do take advantage of the range of prepared vegetables in supermarkets. You will find they are a little more expensive than unprepared vegetables, but their quality is very good and there is absolutely no waste. Most important of all, they save precious time, so it is money well spent. Flavour-packed Mediterranean vegetables are long-term favourites, but try to experiment with some of the more unusual and exotic varieties. Ring the changes by swapping sweet potatoes for ordinary potatoes, different types of squash for courgettes, Chinese leaves or bok choy for cabbage, and Japanese white mooli for red radish. By the same token, serve polenta instead of potatoes, and couscous or bulgur in place of rice or pasta. All are quick and easy to cook, so there is no extra time or trouble involved.

No-cook leafy salads are the quickest of side dishes to serve, but don't just shake the leaves out of the bag and leave it at that. Always add a fresh ingredient or two to give a personal touch. Croûtons and chunks of celery add crunch, strips of sweet pepper give colour, while snipped fresh herbs, roasted peppers and sun-dried tomatoes are full of flavour. A spoonful of crispy lardons, grated cheese or chopped nuts all add protein – each is a simple yet effective addition that can transform an ordinary salad into something special. For a choice of homemade dressings, turn to pages 188-189.

ROASTED MEDITERRANEAN VEGETABLES

THERE IS NOTHING like the chargrilled flavour of roasted vegetables, and yet they are so quick and easy to cook in the oven. They are good served hot as an accompaniment to meat or poultry, or cold as a salad or first course.

2 large peppers (red and yellow)
1 aubergine, weighing about 300 g (10 oz)
2 large courgettes, total weight about 375 g (12 oz)
250 g (8 oz) cherry plum tomatoes
2 large garlic cloves
1–2 fresh thyme sprigs
6 tablespoons olive oil
salt and freshly ground black pepper
extra olive oil and/or balsamic vinegar, to serve (optional)

Serves 4-6

Preparation time: 10 minutes

**Cooking time:
40-50 minutes**

Chef's Tips

Roasted vegetables are delicious cold, mixed with chopped fresh herbs such as basil, thyme, rosemary or marjoram. They are also good with chopped stoned black or green olives.

If you want to reheat them, simply pan-fry in a little olive oil. They make a marvellous filling for pitta pockets, with feta cheese.

1   Preheat the oven to 190°C (375°F) Gas 5. Cut the peppers into chunks, removing the seeds and spongy ribs. Cut off the ends of the aubergine and courgettes, then cut these vegetables into chunks. Remove any hulls from the tomatoes. Roughly chop the garlic.

2   Put the prepared vegetables and thyme sprigs in a roasting tin and sprinkle with the garlic, olive oil and salt and pepper. Stir well to mix. Roast for 40-50 minutes until all the vegetables are tender and charred, stirring several times.

To Serve Sprinkle with extra olive oil and/or balsamic vinegar if you like, and serve hot or cold.

AUBERGINES WITH GARLIC AND ROSEMARY

ITH ITS RICH Mediterranean flavour, this dish of diced aubergines goes well with roast or barbecued lamb. For a Middle Eastern touch, serve topped with a spoonful of thick Greek yogurt.

2 medium to large aubergines
2–3 garlic cloves
1 fresh rosemary sprig
4 tablespoons olive oil
salt and freshly ground black pepper

Serves 4

Preparation time: 10 minutes

Cooking time:
about 12 minutes

Variation

Other herbs, such as thyme, flat-leaf parsley or basil, can be used in addition to, or instead of, the rosemary.

1 Trim the aubergines and cut them into small cubes. Finely chop the garlic. Remove the leaves from the rosemary and finely chop them.

2 Heat the olive oil in a sauté pan, add the aubergines and sauté over moderate heat for about 5 minutes. Season with salt and pepper.

3 Add the chopped garlic and sauté for a further 5 minutes, then stir in the rosemary. Remove from the heat and allow to stand for 1 minute.

To Serve Taste for seasoning, then turn into a warm serving bowl. Serve hot.

CURRIED CAULIFLOWER AND POTATO IN COCONUT MILK

Subtly spiced, this is a good accompaniment for Indian meat or fish curries. It also makes a good vegetarian main course for 2 people, served with basmati rice or Indian bread and Cucumber and Mint Raita (page 152).

2 medium potatoes, total weight about 250 g (8 oz)
250 g (8 oz) cauliflower florets
1 small onion
salt and freshly ground black pepper
1 tablespoon sunflower oil
1 tablespoon curry powder or garam masala
1 teaspoon turmeric
1 teaspoon ground ginger
250 ml (8 fl oz) unsweetened coconut milk

To Serve

a little coconut milk
1–2 tablespoons chopped fresh coriander

Serves 4

Preparation time: 10 minutes

Cooking time:
30-35 minutes

1 Peel the potatoes, then cut them into 2.5 cm (1 inch) cubes. Divide the cauliflower into small sprigs and trim the stalks. Finely chop the onion.

2 Put the potatoes in a pan of salted cold water, bring to the boil and cook for 5 minutes. Remove with a slotted spoon and set aside. Add the cauliflower to the boiling water and cook for 2 minutes. Drain and refresh under the cold tap.

3 Heat the oil in a large saucepan over low to moderate heat. Add the onion and cook gently for 3-5 minutes until softened and lightly coloured. Add the ground spices and stir for 1-2 minutes, then add the potatoes and cook for a further 1-2 minutes, stirring until well coated.

4 Add the coconut milk and 150 ml (¼ pint) water, season to taste and bring to a simmer. Cover and cook for 7-10 minutes. Uncover the pan, add the cauliflower and cook for 3 minutes or until the potatoes and cauliflower are just tender.

To Serve Taste for seasoning, then turn into a warm serving bowl. Drizzle a little coconut milk over the top and sprinkle with chopped coriander. Serve hot.

Chef's Tip

Buy canned coconut milk. It is much more convenient than blocks of creamed coconut, which need to be dissolved in hot water before use. Any leftover coconut milk will keep in a covered bowl in the refrigerator for several days. If you like, you can use it to make coconut rice – just add it to the water when boiling rice in the usual way.

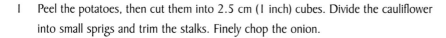

NORMANDY CARROTS

Serves 4

Preparation time: 10 minutes

Cooking time:
about 15 minutes

Chef's Tip

*If using old, mature carrots,
add a pinch or two of sugar
to sweeten them a little.*

Variation

*For extra flavour, add a finely
chopped shallot or small
onion to the carrots before
adding the cider.*

A RICH VEGETABLE DISH, traditionally made with Normandy cider. It is good with plain roast or grilled meat or poultry. Here it is made with sliced carrots, but it can be made equally well with whole baby carrots.

500 g (1 lb) carrots
salt and freshly ground black pepper
200 ml (7 fl oz) dry cider
juice of ½ lemon
20 g (¾ oz) butter
nutmeg
150 ml (¼ pint) double cream
finely chopped fresh flat-leaf parsley, to garnish

1   Peel the carrots and cut them on the diagonal into 5 mm (¼ inch) thick slices. Cook them in salted boiling water for 8 minutes.

2   Drain the carrots and place them in a shallow pan with the cider, lemon juice and butter. Sprinkle with salt and pepper and grate a little nutmeg over them. Bring to a simmer, cover and cook for 5 minutes.

3   Uncover the pan and continue cooking until all the liquid has evaporated and the carrots are covered with a nice glaze. Add the cream and heat through, shaking the pan to coat the carrots with it.

To Serve   Taste for seasoning, turn into a warm serving bowl and sprinkle with chopped parsley. Serve immediately.

VICHY CARROTS

N AMED AFTER THE spa town of Vichy in the Massif Central, these carrots shine with a sweet, buttery glaze. They are good with plain roast or grilled meat and poultry, and children always seem to love them.

500 g (1 lb) carrots
60 g (2 oz) butter
1–2 teaspoons sugar, to taste
salt and freshly ground black pepper

Serves 4

Preparation time: 10 minutes

Cooking time:
about 20 minutes

Variations

After uncovering the pan in step 2, add 60 g (2 oz) currants that have been soaked in cold water for 30 minutes and drained.

For an oriental flavour, add a sprinkling of ground cumin or cumin seeds after taking the lid off the pan, or some grated fresh root ginger. For a sweeter taste, add finely diced stem ginger.

Use young French turnips (navets) instead of carrots.

1   Peel the carrots and cut them into 5 mm (¼ inch) thick slices. Put the slices in a shallow pan with the butter, sugar and salt and pepper to taste. Add just enough water to cover the carrots and bring to the boil. Cover and cook for 10 minutes.

2   Uncover the pan and continue cooking until any remaining liquid has evaporated and the carrots are coated in a nice glaze. Stir occasionally to make sure that the carrots are evenly coated and to keep them from colouring.

To Serve   Taste for seasoning, then turn into a warm serving bowl. Serve hot.

MASHED POTATOES

S MOOTH, CREAMY MASH is effortlessly achieved if you follow this recipe. The secret is to use floury potatoes such as King Edward, Desirée or Pentland Squire, purée them with a ricer or food mill, then beat in hot milk.

1 kg (2 lb) potatoes
salt
200 ml (7 fl oz) milk
30–60 g (1–2 oz) butter

1   Peel the potatoes and cut them lengthways into quarters. Place in a saucepan of salted cold water and bring to the boil, then cover and cook at a medium boil for 15-20 minutes until just tender. Drain and set aside, covered.

2   Bring the milk to the boil and set aside. Mash the potatoes through a ricer or food mill and return them to the saucepan. Beat in the hot milk gradually.

3   Cut the butter into small cubes. Place the puréed potatoes over low heat and stir in the butter cubes using a wooden spoon or spatula. Mix until the butter has completely melted. Taste and add salt if necessary.

To Serve Scoop the mash out of the pan with a large metal spoon (or an ice-cream baller if you like) and serve immediately, while piping hot.

Serves 4

Preparation time: 15 minutes

Cooking time:
25-30 minutes

Variations

Make saffron mash. Cook the potatoes in step 1 with a good pinch of saffron threads or powder.

Make garlic mash. Boil 1-2 peeled garlic cloves with the potatoes, then mash them with the potatoes as in step 2.

Use single or double cream or crème fraîche instead of some of the milk in step 2.

Use 2-3 tablespoons olive oil instead of the butter in step 3.

POLENTA

R INGS OF FRIED polenta make an excellent accompaniment to saucy stews and casseroles, or a tasty side dish to eggs and bacon for brunch. For a first course or snack, they taste superb with a rich tomato sauce.

125 g (4 oz) instant polenta
1 tablespoon grated Parmesan cheese
15 g (½ oz) butter
salt and freshly ground black pepper
olive oil, for frying

Serves 4

Preparation time: 5 minutes, plus cooling and chilling

Cooking time: about 3 minutes

Chef's Tip

Double-check the packet of polenta before buying – instant or pre-cooked polenta cooks in about 3 minutes and is virtually foolproof. Other types can take up to 20 minutes and are difficult to get smooth if you are not used to cooking polenta regularly. The usual amount of water is 500 ml (16 fl oz) to 125 g (4 oz) polenta, but always read the instructions on the packet before you start.

Variation

Top the rings of polenta with sliced goat's cheese or grated Parmesan, Gruyère or Emmenthal, and melt under the grill.

1 Cook the polenta according to the instructions on the packet . Once cooked, mix in the Parmesan and butter, then season to taste. Turn the polenta out onto a sheet of cling film, leave until just cool enough to handle, then roll it into a tight log and twist the ends. Allow to cool completely, then chill in the refrigerator until firm.

2 Unwrap the chilled polenta roll and cut it into 1.25 cm (½ inch) thick slices. Fry in hot olive oil in a non-stick frying pan until golden brown on both sides, turning once. The polenta should be firm and crisp on the outside but moist on the inside.

To Serve Remove from the pan with a fish slice, drain on kitchen paper, then arrange on a warm platter. Serve immediately.

HASH BROWNS

ORIGINALLY FROM THE American South-West, hash browns are now famous all over the world as a brunch dish to serve alongside eggs and bacon. They are also very good with grilled sausages, meat and poultry.

750 g (1½ lb) medium to large floury potatoes
salt and freshly ground black pepper
1 small onion
4 tablespoons sunflower oil
15 g (½ oz) butter

Serves 4

Preparation time: 10 minutes

Cooking time:
35-40 minutes

1 Peel the potatoes and cut them into chunks. Cook in salted boiling water for 15 minutes, then drain and chop. Finely chop the onion.

2 Heat the oil and butter in a shallow non-stick frying pan until hot. Add the onion, stir and cook over low to moderate heat until nicely coloured.

3 Add the chopped potatoes, mix well and shape into a flat cake. Cook over moderate heat until golden brown and crisp underneath, about 15 minutes.

To Serve Invert a warm serving platter over the pan, then turn the platter and pan over so that the golden side of the potato cake is uppermost. Serve immediately, cut into wedges.

Chef's Tip

You can cook the potatoes ahead of time and let them go cold before chopping them.

Variations

Add a chopped green pepper and cook with the onion in step 2.

Add chopped cooked bacon and cook with the potatoes in step 3.

Make corned beef hash. Chop about 125 g (4 oz) corned beef and mix it with the potatoes in step 3.

GRATIN DAUPHINOIS

THIS IS THE PERFECT potato dish for entertaining because it cooks by itself in the oven while you are busy with other things. Here it is made super speedy by using ready prepared potatoes, a trick often used in France.

500 g (1 lb) thinly sliced potatoes
salt and freshly ground black pepper
15 g (½ oz) butter, softened
125 g (4 oz) Emmenthal, Gruyère or Jarlsberg cheese
1 garlic clove
300 ml (½ pint) double cream

1   Preheat the oven to 190°C (375°F) Gas 5. Toss the potatoes in salt and pepper. Brush the inside of an oven-to-table baking dish with the butter and spread the potatoes out in it. Grate the cheese and set aside.

2   Cut the garlic clove in half and place in a saucepan with the cream. Heat just to boiling point and immediately strain over the potatoes. Sprinkle with the grated cheese and bake for 30 minutes.

To Serve Remove from the oven and leave to stand for 5 minutes. Serve straight from the baking dish.

Serves 4

Preparation time: 10 minutes

Cooking time:
about 35 minutes

Chef's Tip

Ready prepared potatoes are sold in vacuum packs or cellophane bags in the fresh chilled sections of most supermarkets. Whole and sliced potatoes are available, and they cook very quickly.

Variation

For potatoes with a beautiful golden glow, add a good pinch of saffron threads or powder to the garlic and cream before scalding.

RICE PILAF

B ASMATI RICE IS given extra flavour and texture with the addition of onion, pistachio nuts and raisins. An ideal accompaniment for Indian curries and other dishes that are cooked in a sauce, it is also good with kebabs and grilled chicken.

1 small onion
90 g (3 oz) shelled pistachio nuts
2 tablespoons olive oil
250 g (8 oz) basmati rice
500 ml (16 fl oz) hot vegetable or chicken stock
salt and freshly ground black pepper
15 g (½ oz) butter
90 g (3 oz) raisins or currants

Serves 4

Preparation time: 5 minutes

Cooking time:
about 30 minutes

1   Finely chop the onion. Shred the pistachios. Heat the oil in a saucepan, add the onion and cook over low heat for 3-5 minutes until softened and lightly coloured.

2   Add the rice and stir for 2-3 minutes until mixed with the onion. Slowly pour in the stock, stir to mix, then bring to the boil. Cover the pan and simmer gently for 20 minutes without lifting the lid.

3   Lift the lid and fork the rice through. Add the butter, pistachios and raisins or currants and fork through until evenly mixed. Season to taste.

To Serve Turn into a warm serving bowl and serve hot.

Chef's Tips

Before cooking basmati rice, read the instructions on the packet. Some varieties need to be rinsed in a sieve under cold running water until the water runs clear. This helps to keep the grains separate.

If you are cooking other things on the top of the stove, you may find it easier to cook the pilaf in the oven. Make it in a flameproof casserole, cover with the lid and cook at 190°C (375°F) Gas 5 for 20 minutes.

Variation

For a touch of colour and spice, add a pinch or two of turmeric or saffron threads or powder after pouring in the stock in step 2.

MUSHROOMS IN GARLIC CREAM

THE PURÉED GARLIC sauce makes these mushrooms wonderfully rich and creamy. They are delicious served with grilled steak or chicken, or tossed with small pasta shapes like penne, farfalle or conchiglie.

6–8 garlic cloves, to taste
400 ml (14 fl oz) hot vegetable or chicken stock
625 g (1¼ lb) button mushrooms
30 g (1 oz) butter
1 teaspoon lemon juice
salt and freshly ground black pepper
200 ml (7 fl oz) double cream

Serves 4

Preparation time: 15 minutes

Cooking time:
about 30 minutes

1 In a small saucepan, gently simmer the whole peeled garlic cloves in the stock until soft, about 18-20 minutes.

2 Meanwhile, finely slice the mushrooms. Melt the butter in a saucepan and add the lemon juice, mushrooms and a pinch of salt. Stir, then cover and simmer over low heat for 10 minutes. Tip the mushrooms into a sieve and reserve the liquid.

3 Put the garlic and stock in a food processor with the mushroom liquid. Blend until smooth. Return to the mushroom pan and boil until reduced and thickened. Add the cream and mushrooms and simmer for 5 minutes, stirring frequently. Season with salt and pepper to taste.

To Serve Turn into a warm serving bowl and serve immediately.

Chef's Tip

For an earthy flavour, use a mixture of cultivated and wild mushrooms. In the autumn when fresh ceps are in season, they are very good cooked in this way.

Variation

For a more intense mushroom flavour, you can add a few dried ceps. These are often sold under their Italian name, porcini. Soak them in warm water for about 20 minutes, then drain them and chop finely. Cook them with the fresh mushrooms in step 2.

ASPARAGUS WITH SOY AND WASABI DRESSING

AN EXCELLENT SALAD for an early summer barbecue party. The distinctive flavour of Japanese wasabi, which is usually served with sushi and sashimi, goes particularly well with barbecued fish.

2 bunches of green asparagus, each weighing about 375 g (12 oz)
salt
1 bunch of spring onions
1–2 tablespoons toasted sesame seeds, to garnish (optional)

Dressing

5 cm (2 inch) piece of fresh root ginger
4 tablespoons soy sauce
juice of 1 lemon
½–1 teaspoon wasabi, to taste
90 ml (3 fl oz) soya oil or other vegetable oil

Serves 6-8

Preparation time:
30-40 minutes

Cooking time: 5 minutes

1 Trim off the woody ends of the asparagus, then scrape or peel the bottom of the spears. Cut each spear into 3 equal pieces, each about 4 cm (1½ inches) long, separating the tips from the stems.

2 Cook the stems in salted boiling water for 3-5 minutes until tender. Remove with a slotted spoon to a colander and refresh under the cold tap. Drain, then leave to dry on kitchen paper. Add the tips to the boiling water and cook for 2 minutes, then drain, refresh and dry as for the stems.

3 Make the dressing. Peel the ginger, grate it into a bowl and add the soy sauce, lemon juice and ½ teaspoon wasabi. Whisk well together, then whisk in the oil a little at a time. Taste and add more wasabi if you like.

4 Thinly slice the spring onions on the diagonal and toss them into the dressing. Add the asparagus stems and turn gently to coat.

To Serve Spoon the asparagus stems in the centre of a serving platter and arrange the tips around the outside. Drizzle some of the dressing from the bowl over the tips. Sprinkle with sesame seeds, if you like. Serve at room temperature.

Chef's Tips

Wasabi is the Japanese version of horseradish, and the mustard-like condiment made from it is available in powder and paste form in Japanese stores and the oriental sections of some supermarkets. The bright green paste sold in tubes is the most convenient form of wasabi; the powder needs to be mixed with water.

Wasabi is at its most powerful when first mixed, but will gradually lose its strength the longer it is exposed to the air.

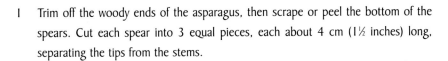

COURGETTES HONGROISE

Serves 4

Preparation time: 10 minutes

Cooking time:
about 25 minutes

Chef's Tip

You can make the sauce several hours in advance. When you are ready to cook the courgettes, bring the sauce to the boil first.

THIS COLOURFUL DISH has a piquant flavour. Serve it with plain grilled or roast meat or poultry. It also makes a very good omelette filling or topping, and can be tossed with pasta for a quick vegetarian supper.

2–3 medium courgettes, total weight about 375 g (12 oz)
½ small onion or 1 shallot
1 small garlic clove
2 tablespoons olive oil
2 teaspoons sweet Hungarian paprika
1 tablespoon tomato purée
300 ml (½ pint) hot vegetable stock or water
salt and freshly ground black pepper

1 Top and tail the courgettes, then cut them into 1.25 cm (½ inch) thick slices. Chop the onion or shallot. Crush the garlic. Heat the oil in a medium saucepan, add the onion and cook over low heat until soft and translucent.

2 Sprinkle in the paprika and cook, stirring, for 30 seconds. Stir in the tomato purée and garlic and cook for 1 minute, then pour in the stock or water, season and bring to the boil, stirring. Cover, then simmer gently for 10 minutes.

3 Add the courgettes and stir to coat in the sauce, then cover and cook over low heat for 10 minutes, stirring 2-3 times to cook and flavour evenly.

To Serve Taste for seasoning, then turn into a warm serving bowl. Serve hot.

GREEN BEANS WITH LEEKS AND TOMATOES

A SPECIAL VEGETABLE DISH to serve with plainly cooked meat or poultry. It goes especially well with roast chicken, and because the beans are coated in sauce there is no need to make gravy.

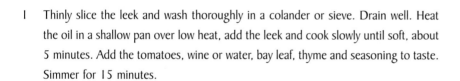

1 leek (white part only)
2 tablespoons olive oil
1 x 400 g can chopped tomatoes
100 ml (3½ fl oz) dry white wine or water
1 bay leaf
2–3 fresh thyme sprigs
salt and freshly ground black pepper
200 g (7 oz) green beans

Serves 4

Preparation time: 10 minutes

Cooking time:
about 30 minutes

1 Thinly slice the leek and wash thoroughly in a colander or sieve. Drain well. Heat the oil in a shallow pan over low heat, add the leek and cook slowly until soft, about 5 minutes. Add the tomatoes, wine or water, bay leaf, thyme and seasoning to taste. Simmer for 15 minutes.

2 Meanwhile, top and tail the beans and blanch them in salted boiling water for 2 minutes. Drain and refresh under cold running water.

3 Add the beans to the tomato sauce and simmer for 3-5 minutes until the beans are tender and the sauce has reduced and is thick. Discard the bay leaf and thyme.

To Serve Taste for seasoning, then turn into a warm serving bowl. Serve hot.

Chef's Tip

You can make the sauce up to 3 days ahead of time and keep it in a covered bowl in the refrigerator. Before you serve the sauce, reheat it until bubbling, then blanch and add the beans.

SPINACH WITH GARLIC, CREAM AND CORIANDER

EVOKE THE AROMA and flavour of France with this wonderful combination of spinach, garlic and cream. French chefs love to cook spinach this way, without water. It is a very quick and successful method.

500 g (1 lb) young tender spinach leaves
2–4 garlic cloves, to taste
60 g (2 oz) butter
1 teaspoon ground coriander
about 4 tablespoons double cream
salt and freshly ground black pepper

Serves 4

Preparation time: 10 minutes

Cooking time: about 10 minutes

1   Wash the spinach well and remove any stalks. Crush the garlic. Melt the butter in a large saucepan, add the spinach and stir over moderate heat for about 5 minutes until the spinach wilts and has released its liquid.

2   Increase the heat to high and add the garlic and coriander. Stir until all of the liquid has evaporated, then add cream and salt and pepper to taste.

To Serve Turn into a warm serving bowl and serve immediately.

Chef's Tip

Fresh spinach can be very gritty and dirty. Save time by buying it ready prepared and washed in bags from the supermarket. This type of spinach is usually labelled 'baby spinach'. It has small tender leaves that have very little tough stalk on them.

Variation

For an Asian flavour, use canned coconut milk instead of cream.

PASTA SALAD WITH MEDITERRANEAN VEGETABLES

THIS TASTY SALAD is perfect for picnics and other al fresco meals. It is best made the day before, to allow time for the different flavours to mingle and mellow, and will keep for 2-3 days in an airtight container in the refrigerator.

1 aubergine, weighing about
   250 g (8 oz)
1 large courgette, weighing about
   250 g (8 oz)
2 large peppers (red and yellow)
2 garlic cloves
4 tablespoons olive oil
125 g (4 oz) dried pasta shapes
1 large handful of fresh basil

Dressing
2 tablespoons bottled or homemade
   red pesto
2 tablespoons balsamic vinegar
salt and freshly ground black pepper
100 ml (3½ fl oz) olive oil

Serves 4-6

Preparation time: 20 minutes,
plus chilling

Cooking time:
40-50 minutes

1 Preheat the oven to 190°C (375°F) Gas 5. Cut the vegetables into large chunks, discarding the cores, seeds and spongy ribs from the peppers. Roughly chop the garlic. Place the vegetables in a roasting tin, add the garlic and olive oil and toss to combine. Roast for 40-50 minutes, turning the vegetables several times.

2 Meanwhile, cook the pasta according to the instructions on the packet. Make the dressing. Place the pesto in a large bowl with the vinegar and 1 tablespoon cold water. Whisk to mix, season to taste with salt and pepper, then whisk in the olive oil.

3 Drain the pasta well, then add it to the bowl of dressing while it is still hot. Toss lightly but thoroughly until all the pasta shapes are coated.

4 When the vegetables are cooked, add them to the pasta and dressing and toss to combine. Set aside until cool, then cover the bowl with cling film and refrigerate for at least 4 hours, preferably overnight.

To Serve Let stand at room temperature for about 1 hour, then mix the salad well to redistribute the dressing. Taste for seasoning. Shred or tear the basil and add to the salad at the last moment. Serve as a side salad, or as a vegetarian first or main course with hot garlic bread.

Chef's Tip

Red pesto is made from sun-dried tomatoes. You can make it yourself as on page 185, or buy it at most supermarkets and delicatessens. It usually comes in a 190 g jar. After opening and using, cover the top of the pesto with a thin film of olive oil, seal the jar and keep it in the refrigerator. Red pesto is excellent tossed with hot cheese-stuffed ravioli for a quick meal, or spread on toasted bread, topped with sliced or grated cheese and popped under the grill.

COUSCOUS SALAD WITH PRAWNS

A MAIN COURSE SALAD that is both colourful and full of flavour. Serve with crusty bread for a summer al fresco meal. For vegetarians or to serve as a side salad, simply omit the prawns.

200 g (7 oz) quick-cooking couscous
2–3 firm tomatoes, total weight about 250 g (8 oz)
2 peppers (red and yellow), each weighing about 150 g (5 oz)
1–2 garlic cloves, to taste
250 g (8 oz) peeled cooked prawns, thawed if frozen
juice of 2 limes
salt and freshly ground black pepper
150 ml (¼ pint) extra-virgin olive oil
1 large handful of fresh coriander or mint

Serves 6

Preparation time:
about 30 minutes

1 Put the couscous in a large bowl and pour boiling water over to cover the grains by about 2.5 cm (1 inch). Leave to soak for about 20 minutes, fluffing up the grains with a fork halfway through.

2 Meanwhile, core, deseed and dice the tomatoes. Place them in a sieve to drain off excess liquid. Deseed the peppers and dice to the same size as the tomatoes. Crush the garlic. Dry the prawns thoroughly on kitchen paper.

3 Make the dressing. Whisk together the lime juice, garlic and salt and pepper until the salt has dissolved. Gradually whisk in the oil until it emulsifies. Finely chop about one-third of the coriander or mint and whisk into the dressing.

4 Roughly chop about three-quarters of the prawns and add to the couscous with the vegetables and dressing. Mix everything together well. Set aside one sprig of the remaining coriander or mint for the garnish, then coarsely chop the rest and mix it into the salad. Chill until serving time.

To Serve Stir the salad well and taste for seasoning, then turn into a serving bowl. Arrange the remaining whole prawns and the reserved herb sprig on top. Serve chilled or at room temperature.

Variations

Use bulgur wheat instead of couscous, preparing it according to the instructions on the packet.

Roasted Peppers (page 184) can be used instead of fresh peppers.

The prawns can be replaced with drained and flaked canned tuna.

Fresh raw scallops or fish can be marinated in the dressing for up to 4 hours, then mixed into the salad instead of the prawns.

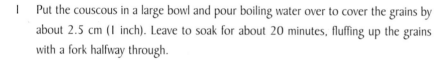

CORN SALAD

Serves 2-3

Preparation time: 10 minutes

Cooking time:
40-50 minutes

Chef's Tip

To save time, you can buy ready roasted peppers, either in a jar or loose at the delicatessen. Or, for a crunchier texture and less smoky flavour, simply use fresh unroasted pepper, which will also save time.

Variations

Drain and flake 1 x 200 g can tuna and fold gently into the salad.

Boil and drain 125 g (4 oz) small pasta shapes, then mix with the vinaigrette while hot. Leave to cool, then add the remaining ingredients. To make a main course salad, you can add canned tuna as suggested above.

A TASTY ACCOMPANIMENT WITH a Mexican flavour that goes well with plain roast or grilled meat or poultry. It's ideal with barbecued food, such as spicy chargrilled drumsticks, steaks, chops or burgers.

1 large red pepper
1 large garlic clove
1 x 340 g can sweetcorn
1 heaped tablespoon chopped fresh coriander
4 tablespoons Balsamic Vinaigrette (page 188), or to taste

1   Preheat the oven to 190°C (375°F) Gas 5. Cut the pepper lengthways into quarters and remove the cores, seeds and spongy ribs. Roast the pepper in the oven for 40-50 minutes until blistered and charred. Place in a plastic bag and set aside to cool, then peel off the skin and dice the flesh. Crush the garlic.

2   Drain the sweetcorn and place in a bowl with the diced roasted pepper, crushed garlic, chopped coriander and vinaigrette. Stir well to mix, then taste and add more vinaigrette if you like.

To Serve Turn into a serving bowl and serve at room temperature.

THREE BEAN SALAD

THIS SIMPLE BUT CLEVER combination of fresh and canned beans makes a colourful and crunchy salad. It can be made all year round, but it is especially useful in winter when leafy salads are not at their best.

150 g (5 oz) French beans
salt
1 x 400 g can red kidney beans
1 x 400 g can chickpeas
4 tablespoons Vinaigrette (page 188)
a little sugar, to taste
1 small red onion, to serve

1   Cut the French beans into 5 cm (2 inch) lengths and cook in salted boiling water for 3-4 minutes until al dente. Drain and rinse under the cold tap.

2   Drain and rinse the canned beans and chickpeas. Drain again and place in a bowl with the French beans and the vinaigrette mixed with sugar to taste. Mix well, cover and refrigerate for about 4 hours or overnight.

To Serve   Toss well and taste for seasoning, then turn into a serving bowl. Finely slice the onion and arrange over the top.

Serves 4-6

Preparation time:
10-15 minutes,
plus chilling

Cooking time:
3-4 minutes

Variations

For a more pungent flavour, add a few tablespoons of chopped fresh coriander and/or some chopped garlic.

For a main course salad, drain and flake 1 x 200 g can tuna and fold gently into the beans just before serving.

Cucumber and Mint Raita

Serves 3-4

Preparation time: 10 minutes, plus draining and chilling

Variations

Fresh coriander can be used in place of mint, or you can use a combination of both.

Chopped garlic can be added to the yogurt with the mint.

Instead of the seaweed garnish, sprinkle chopped fresh mint over the raita just before serving.

C OOL AND REFRESHING, raita is the ideal accompaniment for spicy foods, especially Indian curries, and it is also good with hot Indian bread and pitta bread. It can be made several hours ahead of serving.

½ large cucumber
1 teaspoon salt
90 ml (3 fl oz) natural yogurt
½ tablespoon white wine vinegar
freshly ground black pepper
6 fresh mint leaves
4 tablespoons shredded nori seaweed, to garnish (optional)

1 Peel the cucumber, cut it lengthways in half, then crossways into thin slices. Toss with the salt and place in a colander to drain for 30 minutes.

2 Mix the yogurt and vinegar together and add peppper to taste. Finely shred the mint and stir it into the yogurt mixture.

3 Turn the cucumber into a clean tea towel and press gently to remove excess water. Add to the yogurt and mix well. Chill in the refrigerator for at least 20 minutes before serving.

To Serve Sprinkle with shredded seaweed if you like. Serve chilled.

CELERIAC SALAD

A WINTER SALAD THAT goes well with cooked and smoked meats, especially smoked duck (page 17). In France it is often served as part of an hors d'oeuvre. It also makes a tasty first course served with grated carrots in Vinaigrette (page 188).

1 small celeriac
juice of 1 lemon
salt and freshly ground black pepper
150 ml (¼ pint) mayonnaise

1   Quarter and peel the celeriac, then cut it into pieces that will fit inside the feeder tube of a food processor.

2   Fit the medium or fine grating blade in the processor and grate the celeriac. Place in a bowl and add the lemon juice and salt and pepper to taste. Toss well to mix, add the mayonnaise and toss again.

To Serve Taste for seasoning, then turn into a serving bowl. Cover tightly with cling film and serve as soon as possible or the celeriac may discolour.

Serves 4-6

Preparation time: 10 minutes

Variations

In France, where this salad is called rémoulade, it often has raisins added. Soak about 60 g (2 oz) raisins in cold water for about 30 minutes, then drain and add to the salad at the same time as the mayonnaise.

For a more piquant flavour, add 1-2 teaspoons Dijon or coarse-grained mustard.

Vegetables
quick and easy ideas

Asparagus

• Place asparagus spears lying down in a sauté pan of salted boiling water. Simmer for 5-10 minutes until tender. Drain and serve with warm melted butter. Finely grated lemon rind can be added to the butter, or some very finely chopped fresh dill.

• Brush asparagus spears with olive oil and place on a hot ridged cast iron pan. Chargrill for about 5 minutes, turning once. Serve drizzled with a little extra-virgin olive oil and balsamic vinegar and topped with shavings of Parmesan cheese.

Aubergines

• Pan-fry aubergine slices in very hot olive oil. Drain on kitchen paper and sprinkle with salt. Serve with a bowl of Greek yogurt.

• Make Aubergine Parmigiana, an excellent main course for vegetarians. Layer pan-fried aubergine slices in a baking dish with homemade tomato sauce. Top with sliced mozzarella and grated Parmesan cheese. Bake at 190°C (375°F) Gas 5 for about 30 minutes.

Beans

• Cook trimmed French beans in salted boiling water for 6 minutes. Sweat finely chopped shallots in butter. When the beans are tender, drain thoroughly and toss in the shallot butter. Season with salt and pepper.

• Sprinkle drained cooked beans with crispy bacon bits before serving.

• Toss drained cooked beans in homemade tomato sauce, adding shredded fresh basil leaves and plenty of freshly ground black pepper at the last moment.

Broccoli

• Cook trimmed broccoli florets in salted boiling water for 4 minutes. Drain well and toss with toasted almonds or pine nuts, a knob of butter and salt and pepper.

• Add a few chopped canned anchovies and a little grated lemon rind to cooked broccoli. Toss to combine.

• Stir-fry broccoli florets in sunflower oil with red pepper strips. Sprinkle with sesame oil before serving.

Cabbage

• Cook shredded greens in salted boiling water for 3 minutes. Drain and toss with butter and wholegrain mustard, caraway or cumin seeds.

• Blanch shredded cabbage for 1-2 minutes, drain and stir-fry in a mixture of sunflower and sesame oil. Finish with a dash of soy or chilli sauce.

Carrots

- Cook whole baby carrots or batons in salted boiling water with a pinch of sugar. Allow 6 minutes for whole carrots, 3-4 minutes for batons. Drain, return to pan and glaze with butter and cream or crème fraîche. Sprinkle with black pepper before serving.

Courgettes

- Gently pan-fry courgette slices in olive oil with chopped garlic. Sprinkle with dried breadcrumbs, salt and pepper, and fry over high heat until crispy.

Mushrooms

- Sauté sliced mushrooms in olive oil with finely chopped garlic, ½-1 teaspoon dried herbes de Provence and salt and freshly ground black pepper. Serve sprinkled with lots of finely chopped fresh parsley. If you have any crème fraîche or cream, stir in a few tablespoons.

Parsnips

- Cook peeled chunks of parsnip in salted boiling water for 15-20 minutes until tender. Drain and mash like potatoes with hot milk, butter and seasoning.

- Pare parsnips into ribbons with a vegetable peeler. Stir-fry in hot oil with ribbons of carrot and grated fresh root ginger. Sprinkle with rice wine or balsamic vinegar.

Peas

- Make petits pois à la française. Cook frozen petits pois or peas for 5 minutes in a minimum of salted boiling water with a few letttuce leaves, a knob of butter and a pinch of sugar. Drain and sprinkle with pepper.

- Make petits pois au jambon. Cook frozen petits pois or peas in salted boiling water for 5 minutes, drain and toss with butter and shredded ham.

Peppers

- Roast and peel whole red, orange and yellow peppers (page 184). Cut lengthways into slivers. Arrange in a serving dish and dress with olive oil, lemon juice, crushed garlic and black pepper. Serve cold.

- Quarter red, green and yellow peppers lengthways and deseed. Fill each quarter with a spoonful of pesto and roast at 190°C (375°F) Gas 5 for 30 minutes. Serve hot, topped with shavings of Parmesan cheese.

Potatoes

- Cook new potatoes in salted boiling water with a few sprigs of fresh mint for 15-20 minutes until tender. Drain and return to pan with a good knob of butter. Shake to coat the potatoes in the melting butter, then sprinkle with chopped fresh mint.

- Put small chunks of unpeeled potatoes in a roasting tin with olive oil and whole unpeeled garlic cloves. Roast at 200°C (400°F) Gas 6 for 45 minutes to 1 hour, shaking the tin and turning the potatoes once.

- Cook unpeeled potatoes in salted boiling water for about 20 minutes until tender. Drain, peel off skins and slice potatoes quite thickly. Arrange slices in a baking dish. Sweat finely chopped shallots in butter, add chopped parsley and seasoning and pour over potatoes. Heat through in a hot oven for 5 minutes.

Spinach

- Wash spinach and cook in a large pan with only the water that clings to the leaves. Allow about 5 minutes until wilted, drain and return to pan. Toss over high heat with butter, salt and freshly ground black pepper. Grate fresh nutmeg over the top just before serving.

- Toss drained cooked spinach in a wok with soy sauce, crushed garlic and sesame oil. For a fiery touch, add a little deseeded and chopped fresh chilli.

Desserts

EVERYONE LOVES DESSERT, even if they won't admit it. Chocolate, ice-cream, fresh fruit, pies and tarts, old-fashioned 'nursery' puddings, cheesecakes, crêpes and crumbles – who can resist? So even when you're very busy, take just a little time to plan dessert.

For really quick and easy ideas, turn to pages 178-179. Here you will find suggestions for desserts that you can put together in moments. Clever ways with fresh fruit, creamy concoctions, tart fillings, chocolate and even cheese, both for everyday and special occasions.

With all foods, but particularly with desserts, presentation is the key. A few fresh fruits look beautiful when arranged on a pretty plate or served in a fine glass bowl, a tart made with bought pastry instantly looks better if elevated on a cake stand rather than placed on a flat plate, and a delicate dusting of icing or caster sugar does wonders to lift even the plainest of puddings. Decorations are a must, and even the simplest of finishing touches will add style to your presentation. Sprigs of fresh herbs, strawberries with their neat green hulls, physalis with their caps drawn back, a single swirl of cream – these are all little tricks of the trade used by top chefs to dramatize their desserts.

When you choose to make a full-scale dessert, you will find that most of the recipes in this chapter can be made the day before and kept in the refrigerator until serving time, a real bonus when you are entertaining. They are all very simple and quick, so much so that you will find it easy to offer two desserts, a nice touch if it is a special celebration or you are serving a crowd. Guests appreciate a choice and, even more, the possibility of a second helping, which draws the meal to a relaxed and leisurely close.

ICEBOX CAKE

Serves 6-8

Preparation time: 30 minutes, plus chilling

Chef's Tip

If you can't find ready prepared mango slices, you will need 1 medium mango to give 250 g (8 oz) flesh without the skin and stone.

Variation

Use sponge fingers (boudoir biscuits) instead of trifle sponges. You will need 18-20, depending on the shape of your loaf tin – some tins are not straight sided.

A N AMERICAN DESSERT, so called because 'icebox' was the original word for refrigerator. It needs to chill for at least 8 hours before serving, so it is the perfect dessert to make the day before a dinner party.

1 x 250 g (8 oz) punnet ripe strawberries
450 ml (¾ pint) double cream
1 x 250 g (8 oz) tub fresh mango slices
1 x 125 g (4 oz) punnet ripe raspberries
8 trifle sponges
4 tablespoons kirsch or brandy

1   Brush a 23 x 12.5 cm (9 x 5 inch) loaf tin very lightly with oil, then line with cling film, letting it overhang the sides. Set aside 6-8 whole strawberries and about 4 tablespoons of the cream for the decoration.

2   Hull and finely chop the remaining strawberries. Drain and finely chop the mango slices. Put the whole raspberries in a bowl, add the chopped fruit and stir to mix. Whip the remaining cream until thick but not buttery.

3   Place 4 trifle sponges side by side in the bottom of the loaf tin and sprinkle with half the kirsch or brandy. Cover with half the fruit mixture, then spread half the whipped cream over the fruit.

4   Repeat the layers, then cover with the overhanging cling film. Chill in the refrigerator for at least 8 hours, preferably overnight.

To Serve   Run a palette knife between the cling film and the loaf tin, then unfold the cling film on the top and invert the cake onto a plate. Remove the tin and cling film. Whip the reserved cream and spread it over the top of the cake. Halve the reserved strawberries lengthways and place them cut-side down on the cream.

ETON MESS

What could be more English than strawberries and cream? This is a variation that was supposedly created at Eton, when the strawberries were overripe and too soft to serve whole.

2 x 250 g (8 oz) punnets ripe strawberries
2 tablespoons Cointreau
300 ml (½ pint) double or whipping cream
60 g (2 oz) ready made meringue

1   Wash the strawberries and set aside the 6 best ones for decoration. Hull the rest of the strawberries and put them in a large bowl. Add the Cointreau and crush the strawberries lightly with a fork.

2   Whip the cream until it is thick enough to leave a ribbon trail. Fold it into the crushed strawberry and Cointreau mixture.

3   With your hands, lightly crush two-thirds of the meringue over the strawberry and cream mixture. Gently fold the meringue in with a rubber spatula or large metal spoon until it is evenly mixed.

To Serve   Pile into 6 glass dishes or wine glasses and crush the remaining meringue over the top. Serve decorated with the reserved strawberries, using them whole, halved or fanned out.

Serves 6

Preparation time: 15 minutes

Chef's Tips

This dessert was created for strawberries that are past their best, so only use really ripe fruit. It is intended to be eaten straight after making, but can be kept in the refrigerator for several hours before serving.

You can buy ready made individual meringue nests, large meringue baskets and pavlova shells in boxes in supermarkets. They are all equally suitable for this recipe, but try to get the best quality. Some bought meringues, especially the snowy white ones, are too sugary sweet.

Variation

Ripe raspberries can be used instead of strawberries. They do not need to be crushed.

CHOCOLATE VACHERIN

THIS SIMPLE TRICK of artful assembly is bound to impress your guests, and it takes no time at all to do. For an extra touch of luxury, pipe melted dark chocolate onto each plate before serving, as shown in the photograph.

1 litre (1¾ pints) chocolate ice-cream
2 x 90 g packets meringue nests
1 heaped teaspoon cocoa powder, to finish

Serves 8

Preparation time:
10-15 minutes

Chef's Tip

You can use any ice-cream or sorbet you like. If you use a fruit flavour, dust the top of the vacherin with icing sugar rather than cocoa powder.

Buy ready made meringues from a good retailer or you will be disappointed with the result. Cheap meringues tend to be snowy white and very hard, and can taste quite synthetic.

1   Allow the ice-cream to soften slightly at room temperature. Roughly crush the meringues with your hands.

2   Place about one-third of the meringue in a layer over the bottom of a 23 cm (9 inch) springform cake tin. Spread with half the ice-cream, pressing it down well with the back of a metal spoon or a small palette knife.

3   Cover with another layer of meringue, then spread with the remaining ice-cream. Top with the remaining meringue and freeze until ready to serve.

To Serve Run a palette knife between the vacherin and the tin, then unclip the side of the tin and lift off. Sift cocoa powder over the top layer of meringue, then transfer the vacherin to a cake stand or serving plate. Serve at once, in generous slices.

LEMON CHEESECAKE

T HE PERFECT CHEESECAKE — rich and creamy, with a tangy kick from the lemon rind and juice. You can serve it plain, with thick pouring cream, or top it with seasonal fruits. It looks and tastes especially good with soft summer berries.

6 digestive biscuits
3 tablespoons caster sugar
30 g (1 oz) butter, melted
500 g (1 lb) cream cheese
150 g (5 oz) caster sugar
2 large eggs
grated rind and juice of 1 lemon
icing sugar, to serve

Serves 6-8

Preparation time: 20 minutes, plus chilling

Cooking time: 40 minutes

Variations

Use lime or orange instead of lemon and, if using orange, add 4 tablespoons finely ground toasted hazelnuts. Gingersnaps or chocolate chip cookies can be used instead of digestive biscuits, or you can reduce the amount of digestive biscuits and make up the weight with chopped nuts. If making a chocolate crust, melt 60 g (2 oz) unsweetened chocolate and add it to the filling with 4 tablespoons frangelico or amaretto liqueur. For a fruity filling, mix about 175 g (6 oz) frozen blueberries into the filling before baking. For a marbled filling, flavour one-third of the mixture with chocolate or coffee and swirl it in.

1   Preheat the oven to 170°C (325°F) Gas 3. Butter the inside of a 20 cm (8 inch) springform cake tin. Crush the biscuits finely in a food processor, mix in the sugar, then the melted butter. Press the mixture firmly into the bottom of the tin. Set aside.

2   Make the filling. Beat the cream cheese with an electric whisk to soften it, then add the sugar and beat well. Add the eggs one at a time and finally add the lemon rind and juice. Beat well to combine.

3   Pour the filling into the prepared tin, level the surface and bake for 40 minutes. Remove from the oven and allow to cool completely, then refrigerate for at least 4 hours, preferably longer.

To Serve Unclip the side of the tin and remove. Slide a palette knife between the bottom of the cheesecake and the tin and carefully lift the cheesecake off the metal base onto a serving plate. Sift icing sugar over the top just before serving.

White chocolate and cream cheese tart

A SENSATIONAL-LOOKING DESSERT that is unbelievably simple to make, especially if you use ready rolled frozen pastry. The combination of cream cheese and white chocolate is wonderful, but your guests will find it difficult to guess what it is.

1 sheet frozen shortcrust pastry, about 28 cm (11 inches) in diameter, thawed
400 g (14 oz) cream cheese
125 g (4 oz) caster sugar
1 x 150 g (5 oz) bar good-quality white chocolate

To Serve

about 90 g (3 oz) ripe berries
a little caster sugar

1   Preheat the oven to 190°C (375°F) Gas 5. Put a baking sheet in the oven to heat. Line a 24.5 cm (9½ inch) loose-bottomed metal tart tin with the sheet of pastry and trim the edge. Line the pastry with foil and fill with baking beans. Place on the hot baking sheet and bake blind for 10 minutes. Remove the beans and foil and bake the empty tart shell for 5 minutes. Remove the tart shell from the oven and set it aside to cool in its tin on a wire rack.

2   Meanwhile, beat the cream cheese and sugar together until light and fluffy. Break the chocolate into pieces and place in a heatproof bowl. Set over a saucepan of hot water until melted. Stir into the cream cheese.

3   Spread the cream cheese mixture evenly in the pastry case and leave in a cool place until set, about 1 hour.

To Serve Top with berries, sift caster sugar over and serve immediately.

Serves 6-8

Preparation time: 15 minutes, plus setting

Cooking time: 15 minutes

Chef's Tips

If you prefer to make your own sweet shortcrust pastry, there is a recipe on page 190.

You can make the tart up to 24 hours in advance and keep it loosely covered in a cold place. Add the berries just before serving or juice may weep into the filling and spoil its appearance. Halved small strawberries look good arranged cut-side down in a regular pattern, or you can simply toss together smaller fruit like raspberries and blueberries and pile them on top of the tart.

CHOCOLATE CUPS

Serves 8

Preparation time:
about 30 minutes, including
setting

Chef's Tips

*Chocolate dessert cups
can be bought in boxes at
many supermarkets and
delicatessens. Made from
good-quality dark chocolate,
they are not too sweet.*

*Instead of the chocolate
ganache filling used here,
you can fill the cups with
fresh cream, chocolate
mousse, crème pâtissière
(pastry cream) or ice-cream.*

These dainty little tartlets look sensational. They make very good petits fours to serve with coffee after dinner. Using ready made chocolate cups means that they can be assembled in minutes – perfect for last-minute entertaining.

200 g (7 oz) good-quality dark chocolate
100 ml (3½ fl oz) double cream
8 dark chocolate dessert cups

To Serve

150 g (5 oz) ripe raspberries
1–2 teaspoons icing sugar

1   Make the ganache filling. Break or chop the chocolate into pieces and melt gently in a heatproof bowl over a pan of barely simmering water. Take care not to let the base of the bowl touch the water or the chocolate will scorch. Remove the bowl from the pan.

2   Heat the cream in a small pan until hot, then pour onto the melted chocolate. Stir until evenly mixed, smooth and glossy.

3   Spoon the ganache filling into the chocolate cups and leave to set. This will take 15-20 minutes, depending on the room temperature. If not serving immediately, cover the filled cups and keep them in the refrigerator.

To Serve   Gently press the raspberries into the ganache filling, arranging them with their pointed ends facing upwards. Sift icing sugar evenly over the raspberries and serve at room temperature.

CHOCOLATE AND PECAN YOGURT ICE-CREAM

SING YOGURT AS a base for ice-cream is a short cut well worth knowing. It saves a lot of preparation time, yet the result is just as good as ice-cream made with a custard or cream base. It's healthier too.

60 g (2 oz) good-quality dark chocolate
60 g (2 oz) pecan nuts
1 x 500 g carton natural bio yogurt
60 g (2 oz) caster sugar
1 large egg white
½ teaspoon vanilla extract

Serves 4-6

Preparation time: 20 minutes,
plus freeezing

1   Finely grate the chocolate. Chop the pecans.

2   Mix all the ingredients together and churn in an ice-cream maker until firm. The freezing time will vary according to your machine – some take as little as 20 minutes. If you do not have an electric ice-cream maker, whisk the mixture well in a bowl, then pour into a freezer container. Place in the freezer until beginning to freeze (about 4 hours), then whisk or stir briskly with a fork and return to the freezer. Repeat this process twice more, then freeze until firm.

To Serve Scoop into glasses or bowls and serve immediately.

Chef's Tips

The pecans should not be chopped too coarsely or they will prevent the ice-cream maker from working properly.

Organic bio yogurt and full-fat yogurt are best for ice-cream making. They have a lovely creamy texture.

If the ice-cream has been made or stored in the freezer you may need to soften it at room temperature for 10-15 minutes before serving.

PLUM AND CINNAMON CRUMBLE

Serves 6-8

Preparation time: 20 minutes

Cooking time:
25-30 minutes

Variations

For apple crumble, use Granny Smith apples cut into 5 mm (¼ inch) slices and the finely grated rind and juice of ½ lemon instead of cinnamon. Or use half apples and half cranberries or blackberries.

For a crunchier topping, add 15 g (½ oz) roughly chopped nuts (eg walnuts, hazelnuts, pecans) with the sugar.

Strawberries and blueberries also make excellent crumbles; so too does well-drained canned fruit or thawed frozen fruit. Good choices are pears, gooseberries, rhubarb (with a little chopped stem ginger), peaches and apricots.

A TRADITIONAL FAMILY FAVOURITE. A crumble is quicker and easier to make than a fruit pie or tart, yet equally as popular, especially for Sunday lunch. Plums and cinnamon are a winning combination.

750 g (1½ lb) ripe red plums
60 g (2 oz) caster or demerara sugar
1 teaspoon ground cinnamon

Topping

250 g (8 oz) plain flour
150 g (5 oz) butter, chilled
40 g (1½ oz) caster or demerara sugar

1 Preheat the oven to 190°C (375°F) Gas 5. Halve and stone the plums and place them skin-side up in a large baking dish. Mix the caster or demerara sugar and cinnamon together and sprinkle over the plums.

2 Make the topping. Put the flour in a bowl, cut the butter into 1.25 cm (½ inch) cubes and add to the flour. Rub it in with your fingertips, using a light action, until the mixture resembles fine breadcrumbs and a few small lumps come together (this can also be done in a food processor). Toss in the sugar and mix through evenly.

3 Scatter the crumble mixture evenly over the filling and bake for 25-30 minutes until golden brown.

To Serve Spoon into bowls and serve with cream, custard or fromage frais.

ROASTED FRUIT WITH MASCARPONE CREAM

HOT FRUIT AND chilled cream make a sensational partnership, and an excellent choice for a winter or Christmas dinner party. Serve with a sweet dessert wine such as Muscat de Beaumes de Venise.

1 kg (2 lb) prepared fresh seasonal fruit
60 g (2 oz) butter
60 g (2 oz) walnut pieces
60 g (2 oz) soft brown sugar

Mascarpone Cream

finely grated rind of 1 large orange
juice of 2 large oranges
2–3 cardamom pods
250 g (8 oz) mascarpone cheese, well chilled

Serves 6

Preparation time:
20-30 minutes

Cooking time: 20 minutes

Chef's Tip

Choose firm-textured but ripe fruit. You can use just one or two fruits or several. For a total prepared weight of 1 kg (2 lb), try the following combination: 2 pears and 1 large dessert apple, both quartered, cored and cut into thick slices; 6 dessert plums, halved and stoned; 1 large mango, peeled, stoned and cut into cubes; 200 g (7 oz) prepared pineapple chunks and 6 fresh figs, halved. If using figs, add them when the other fruit are turned over halfway through cooking.

1 First make the mascarpone cream. Put the orange rind and juice in a small pan. Crush the cardamom pods and add the pods and seeds to the pan. Boil gently until syrupy and reduced to about 3-4 tablespoonfuls. Strain and leave to cool, then stir into the mascarpone. Transfer to a small serving bowl, cover with cling film and chill in the refrigerator until ready to serve.

2 Preheat the oven to 200°C (400°F) Gas 6. Spread the fruit out in an even layer in a large baking dish. Melt the butter in a small pan, mix in the nuts and sugar, then drizzle over the fruit. Bake for 10 minutes.

3 Remove the dish from the oven and carefully turn the fruit over. Return the dish to the oven and bake for another 10 minutes or until each piece of fruit is just tender and the syrup is bubbling hot.

To Serve Transfer the fruit to a large serving bowl or individual bowls and serve hot, with the chilled mascarpone cream handed separately.

CRÊPES SUZETTE

USUALLY FLAMBÉED AT the table in restaurants, Crêpes Suzette is quite difficult for the home cook to serve. Here is a really clever alternative that is both simple to prepare and serve, especially if you use ready made French crêpes.

140 g (4½ oz) butter, softened
90 g (3 oz) caster sugar
finely grated rind of 1 large orange
3 tablespoons Cointreau
8 ready made crêpes
200 ml (7 fl oz) orange juice (2 large oranges)

Serves 4-6

Preparation time: 15 minutes

Cooking time: 5-8 minutes

1   Preheat the oven to 220°C (425°F) Gas 7. Brush the inside of a large baking dish with 1 tablespoon of the butter. Put the remaining butter in a bowl and add 60 g (2 oz) of the sugar, the orange rind and 1 tablespoon of the Cointreau. Beat with a wooden spoon until smooth.

2   Take 1 crêpe and spread it thinly with some of the flavoured butter. Fold it in half and spread with another layer of butter. Fold it in half again to make a triangle, then place it in the dish. Repeat with the remaining crêpes and flavoured butter, placing them in the dish as they are done so that each one slightly overlaps the other.

3   Melt the remaining flavoured butter and pour it over the crêpes, then sprinkle with the remaining sugar. Bake for 5-8 minutes or until the crêpes are bubbling hot and the sugar on top is lightly caramelized.

4   Meanwhile, bring the orange juice and the remaining Cointreau to the boil in a small saucepan.

To Serve Remove the dish from the oven, pour the hot orange juice and Cointreau mixture over the crêpes and serve immediately.

Chef's Tip

Traditional sweet crêpes from Brittany are sold in many supermarkets. They are often quite large, about 30 cm (12 inches) in diameter, and are sold in packets of eight. If you make your own crêpes, they are likely to be smaller in size than the ready made French ones, so you will need 12 crêpes for 4-6 people. A recipe for crêpes is given on page 190.

RASPBERRY FOOL

AN ENGLISH CLASSIC, this fool can be made in minutes with fresh, simple ingredients from the supermarket. Rich and creamy, it is best served with light, crisp biscuits such as langues-de-chat or sponge fingers.

750 g (1½ lb) fresh or frozen raspberries
2–3 tablespoons caster sugar, or to taste
a few drops of lemon juice
300 ml (½ pint) prepared custard
300 g (10 oz) fromage frais
a few fresh raspberries, to serve

Serves 4

Preparation time:
15-20 minutes, plus chilling

1   Purée the raspberries in a food processor or blender, then sieve the purée to remove most of the seeds. Taste and add sugar and lemon juice to sweeten and accentuate the flavour of the fruit.

2   In a large bowl, mix together the custard and fromage frais. Stir in the raspberry purée until blended, or blend in half and streak the remainder through.

3   Spoon into 4 wine glasses or champagne flutes and chill in the refrigerator for at least 2 hours.

To Serve   Top each serving with a few raspberries and serve chilled.

Chef's Tips

Strawberries can be used instead of raspberries, and canned fruit such as rhubarb or gooseberries also works well. To make the amount of fruit purée required for this recipe, drain the liquid from 2 x 539 g cans of fruit, then blend the fruit in a food processor or blender.

You can make the fools up to 24 hours in advance and keep them, tightly covered with cling film, in the refrigerator. Top with fresh raspberries before serving.

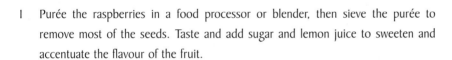

FRAGRANT FRUIT SALAD

Serves 6-8

Preparation time:
30 minutes, plus cooling
syrup and final chilling

Chef's Tip

*Ready prepared mango is an
absolute boon for the busy
cook because the whole fruit
is very fiddly to prepare.
Most supermarkets sell it
in the chilled fruit section.
Check that it is packed in
natural juice rather than a
sweetened syrup.*

D ELICATE AND REFRESHING, this is the perfect dessert to serve after a rich main
course. It uses fruits that are good in winter, when soft fruits and berries are
not at their best.

2 pink grapefruit

2 oranges

4 kiwi fruit

2 x 250 g (8 oz) tubs fresh mango slices

2 pears or dessert apples

juice of 1 lemon

2 tablespoons Cointreau

2 medium bananas

fresh mint sprigs, to serve

Spiced Sugar Syrup

150 g (5 oz) granulated sugar

1 cinnamon stick

1 cardamom pod, split

1 star anise or clove

1   First make the spiced sugar syrup. Put all the ingredients in a saucepan and add
150 ml (¼ pint) water. Bring to the boil. When the sugar has dissolved, immediately
remove from the heat, cover and set aside to cool.

2   Peel and segment the grapefruit and oranges, catching the juice over a large bowl.
Cut the segments into bite-sized pieces. Peel and slice the kiwi fruit and cut each
slice in half. Drain the mango and cut each slice crossways into three. Peel and core
the pears or apples and slice them into bite-sized pieces.

3   Put all the prepared fruit in the bowl with the grapefruit and orange juice and add
the lemon juice. Strain the cool sugar syrup over (you may not need all of it), add
the Cointreau and stir gently to mix. Cover and chill for several hours.

To Serve   Peel and thinly slice the bananas, then cut each slice in half and add to
the fruit salad. Decorate with mint sprigs and serve immediately.

Ginger crème brûlée

Serves 6

Preparation time: 20 minutes, plus cooling and chilling

Cooking time: 30 minutes

Variations

For Cardamom Crème Brûlée, infuse the cream and milk with 3 crushed cardamom pods instead of the fresh root ginger, and use 90 g (3 oz) sugar instead of 125 g (4 oz). Leave the stem ginger in or omit it.

For Vanilla Crème Brûlée, split a vanilla pod in half lengthways and scrape the seeds into the cream and milk before scalding. Leave the chocolate and stem ginger in or omit them.

V ELVETY AND RICH, with a spicy kick from the ginger, this is a dessert for a special occasion. It is best well chilled, so make it the day before serving and keep it in the refrigerator until the last moment. The brûlée topping will stay crisp.

60 g (2 oz) drained stem ginger in syrup
200 ml (7 fl oz) double cream
200 ml (7 fl oz) milk
1–2 slices peeled fresh root ginger, about 15 g (½ oz)
125 g (4 oz) good-quality white chocolate
5 large egg yolks
125 g (4 oz) caster sugar
6 tablespoons demerara sugar

1   Preheat the oven to 150°C (300°F) Gas 2. Finely chop the stem ginger and sprinkle it in the bottom of six 125-150 ml (4-5 fl oz) ramekins. Stand the ramekins in a roasting tin. Put the cream, milk and root ginger in a saucepan and bring just to boiling point. Remove from the heat. Break the chocolate into small pieces and add it to the pan a few pieces at a time, stirring after each addition until melted.

2   In a bowl, whisk together the egg yolks and caster sugar until light in colour. Pour the hot liquid onto them and stir well. Strain into a jug, then pour into the ramekins. Pour enough hot water into the roasting tin to come halfway up the sides of the ramekins. Bake for 30 minutes, until barely set. Turn the oven off and leave the custards to cool in the oven, then cover and refrigerate for at least 4 hours.

3   Preheat the grill to high. Sprinkle the top of each dessert with 1 tablespoon demerara sugar and caramelize for 2-3 minutes. Leave to cool and set, then refrigerate until serving time.

To Serve   Stand the ramekins on small plates or saucers and serve chilled. Each guest should crack open the crisp caramel with a teaspoon to reveal the rich yellow cream underneath.

BANANA TART TATIN

U PSIDE-DOWN HOT fruit tarts are sweet and juicy, and very popular. This is an easy recipe in which everything is done in just one pan. Serve with a chilled cream like crème fraîche, or scoops of vanilla ice-cream.

200 g (7 oz) caster sugar
1 teaspoon lemon juice
4 tablespoons double cream
250–300 g (8–10 oz) ready made puff pastry
6 medium bananas

Serves 4-6

Preparation time: 30 minutes, plus chilling

Cooking time: 30-35 minutes

1   Put the sugar, lemon juice and 4 tablespoons cold water in a heavy frying pan with an ovenproof handle. The pan should measure about 23 cm (9 inches) across the base. Place the pan over moderate heat and stir until the sugar has completely dissolved. Bring to the boil and boil rapidly until the syrup turns a golden caramel colour. Immediately remove from the heat and carefully stir in the cream. Continue stirring, off the heat, until a smooth caramel forms. Set aside to cool.

2   Roll out the pastry to a thickness of about 3 mm (⅛ inch). Cut out a large circle, about 30 cm (12 inches) in diameter, or the same diameter as the top of your frying pan. Prick the pastry all over with a fork.

3   Peel the bananas and trim off the ends. Cut the bananas into 2 cm (¾ inch) cylinders and stand them upright side by side in a single layer in the caramel sauce. Carefully place the puff pastry on top of the bananas, then put the pan in the refrigerator for 30 minutes. Meanwhile, preheat the oven to 200°C (400°F) Gas 6.

4   Bake the tart in the oven for about 30-35 minutes or until the pastry is well risen, golden and cooked through.

To Serve   Place a large flat serving plate upside-down on top of the frying pan. Wearing oven gloves and holding both pan and plate tightly together, carefully invert both so that the tart is on the plate. Lift off the frying pan.

Chef's Tips

For speed, buy fresh puff pastry from the chilled section of the supermarket. Frozen puff pastry is just as good, but you have to wait several hours for it to thaw before you can roll it out.

If your frying pan does not have an ovenproof handle, wrap the handle in several thicknesses of foil. This will protect it from the intense heat of the oven.

LEMON TART

SHARP AND TANGY, this classic French tart is amazingly quick to make, especially when you use a ready rolled sheet of shortcrust pastry to make the tart shell. It is good served perfectly plain, or with cream and berries as shown here.

1 sheet frozen shortcrust pastry, about 28 cm (11 inches in diameter), thawed
6 large eggs
200 ml (7 fl oz) lemon juice (4–6 large lemons)
200 g (7 oz) caster sugar
125 g (4 oz) butter

To Serve

icing sugar
cream
fresh berries

Serves 6-8

Preparation time: 15 minutes, plus chilling

Cooking time: 15 minutes

1   Preheat the oven to 190°C (375°F) Gas 5. Put a baking sheet in the oven to heat. Line a 24.5 cm (9½ inch) loose-bottomed metal tart tin with the sheet of pastry and trim the edge. Line the pastry with foil and fill with baking beans. Place on the hot baking sheet and bake blind for 10 minutes. Remove the beans and foil and bake the empty tart shell for 5 minutes. Remove the tart shell from the oven and set it aside to cool in its tin on a wire rack.

2   Meanwhile, put the eggs, lemon juice and sugar in a saucepan and whisk well. Place over low to moderate heat and whisk constantly with a balloon whisk until thick enough for traces to be left by the whisk when lifted. Remove from the heat and strain into a clean bowl. Dice the butter and mix into the filling until melted.

3   Pour the filling into the pastry case and set aside to cool. Refrigerate for 1-2 hours or until the filling has set.

To Serve   Remove the tart from the refrigerator, carefully remove the tart tin and set the tart on a serving plate. Leave to stand at room temperature for about 30 minutes, then sift icing sugar over the top. Serve with cream and fresh berries.

Chef's Tips

Boxes of round shortcrust pastry sheets are sold in the freezer cabinets of most supermarkets. They are rolled up individually, and need to be thawed before unrolling. The pastry is thin, crisp and light, perfect for making French-style tarts and quiches, but if you prefer to make your own, there is a recipe for sweet shortcrust pastry on page 190.

For baking pastry blind, you can buy ceramic and metal baking beans at kitchenware shops, or use dried pulses or rice. Another way to bake blind is to put a cake tin on top of the foil inside the tart shell. Choose a tin that is slightly smaller in diameter than the tart tin.

Desserts
quick and easy ideas

Fresh Fruit

- Sprinkle sliced mango or papaya with orange juice and a splash of Cointreau. Top with toasted shredded coconut if you like.

- Toss raspberries or loganberries with caster sugar and sprinkle with kirsch. Decorate with fresh mint sprigs.

- Sprinkle chunks or rings of pineapple with kirsch or rum.

- Halve or slice strawberries and sprinkle with a little balsamic vinegar. Turn the fruit gently in the vinegar.

- Grind black pepper lightly over halved or sliced strawberries. Sweeten to taste with caster sugar.

- Combine red fruit – cherries, raspberries, strawberries, blueberries – and toss in vanilla sugar. Or macerate in Cointreau and sugar. Serve well chilled.

- Heat sliced strawberries with butter, sugar, a splash of Cointreau and ½ teaspoon crushed green peppercorns.

- Macerate halved seedless grapes in whisky, honey and lemon juice in the refrigerator overnight. Serve chilled, with crème fraîche.

- Make frudités. Arrange a selection of fresh seasonal fruit on a platter and serve with a bowl of sweetened cream or fromage frais for dipping. Or mix the cream half and half with fromage frais, or with mascarpone cheese, Greek yogurt or soured cream.

- Stir-fry mixed fresh fruit in a little sunflower oil, sprinkle with a little ground ginger, cardamom or five-spice powder. Serve hot, with chilled cream or Greek yogurt.

- Halve bananas lengthways and pan-fry in butter, brown sugar and orange or lime juice, or both. For a spicy flavour, add a pinch of ground cinnamon, cardamom or mixed spice. For a Caribbean kick, add a splash of rum. Serve hot, with vanilla ice-cream.

- Pan-fry apple slices in butter and sugar. Sprinkle with ground cinnamon before serving.

- Make Cherries Jubilee. Heat canned cherries in natural juice with brandy and pour over vanilla ice-cream.

- Make Peach Melba. Purée raspberries in a food processor, then sieve and sweeten to make a coulis. Slice peaches and fan out on individual plates. Top with vanilla ice-cream and pour raspberry coulis over the top.

- Put a few raspberries in the bottom of champagne flutes. Fill flutes with chilled champagne and serve immediately.

Creamy Concoctions

• Fold together whipped cream and Greek yogurt. Layer in wine glasses with sliced or chopped fresh fruit, fruit purée or chopped nuts. Serve chilled.

• Whizz fromage frais or Quark in a food processor with fresh raspberries or strawberries, caster sugar and lemon juice to taste. Spoon into glasses, chill and serve topped with a single fresh fruit.

• Make syllabub. Whip double or whipping cream with a few tablespoons each of sweet white wine and caster sugar and 1-2 teaspoons finely grated orange or lemon rind. Spoon into tall glasses and serve well chilled. If you like, fold soft summer fruit like raspberries and chopped strawberries, peaches, nectarines or apricots into the syllabub. Or add chopped stem ginger.

• Cut a cross in the tops of fresh figs, open them out and fill with cream cheese or ricotta cheese sweetened with caster sugar.

• Fill bought meringue nests with sweetened whipped cream or a mixture of cream and fromage frais or Greek yogurt. Top with berries or sliced fruit, then cut passion fruit in half and scoop their flesh out onto the fruit and cream.

Chocolate

• Top warm brownies with scoops of vanilla ice-cream and drizzle with chocolate sauce. Sprinkle chopped pecans or walnuts over the sauce if you like.

• Scoop chocolate ice-cream into ready made meringue nests, drizzle with chocolate sauce and sprinkle with finely chopped pistachio nuts.

• Make a chocolate fondue by gently melting together equal weights of chocolate and double cream. You can use dark or white chocolate. Pour into a fondue pot and serve with chunks of fresh fruit, sponge fingers or cubes of sponge cake. Use fondue forks for spearing and dipping.

• Make a chocolate sauce by heating together 250 g (8 oz) good-quality dark chocolate, broken into pieces, with 300 ml (½ pint) double cream. Stir in 1 teaspoon rum, Cointreau or peppermint essence if you like. Use as a warm sauce over ice-cream, bananas and crêpes.

• Spear pieces of fresh fruit on cocktail sticks and dip in melted chocolate. Leave to set on baking parchment before serving as petits fours. For a pretty presentation, dip only half of each piece of fruit, or just a corner.

Fillings for Tarts

• Using a shortcrust pastry sheet, make a tart shell and bake it blind as in the recipe for Lemon Tart (page 177). Leave to cool, then fill with one of the following:

• Cream cheese, low-fat soft cheese or Quark sweetened with caster sugar. Stud the cheese filling with blueberries or raspberries, or a mixture of both fruit, arranging them attractively in concentric circles or wedges. If you like, coat with a red glaze made by boiling red jam with a little lemon juice. Sieve, then spoon over fruit.

• Ready made thick custard topped with peach halves placed cut-side down. Decorate between the peaches with shredded pistachios or toasted flaked almonds, then coat with an apricot glaze if you like. Boil apricot jam with a little lemon juice, then sieve and spoon over fruit.

And for the cheese course…

• Many people prefer fruit and cheese to dessert. The following combinations are good:
- Pears with Gorgonzola
- Figs with mascarpone
- Peaches with Dolcelatte
- Dainty fingers of rich fruit cake with Cheddar or Wensleydale
- Crisp apples with blue Stilton, Emmenthal or Gruyère
- Apricots with white Stilton
- Red or green grapes with Brie or Camembert

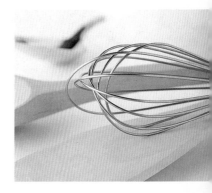

The Basics

JUST ABOUT EVERYTHING can be bought ready made these days, even the most exotic of ingredients. If not in the supermarket, you will find what you are looking for in a delicatessen or ethnic grocery store. Buy the very best quality you can afford: even the greatest chefs are only as good as their ingredients. That said, for the keen cook with a hectic lifestyle, items like ready made dressings, sauces, pastes and marinades – even pastry and crêpes – are a huge help in cutting down on preparation time. In this chapter you will find a handy checklist of useful items to keep in your storecupboard, refrigerator or freezer, all of which feature in recipes in this book.

The secret of good cooking in a minimal amount of time lies in the clever combining of top quality store-bought items with fresh ingredients. If you have a good stock of items like bottled sauces and dressings, spice mixes and flavoured butters, then all you have to do to put together quick and delicious meals is buy a few fresh ingredients when you need them, which will take you hardly any time and even less effort.

The recipes in this chapter are for times when you prefer to make your own basics, or when you have run out of stock in your storecupboard. You can even stock up with homemade basics, because storage instructions and times are given with all the recipes where possible. A homemade dressing or marinade will not only taste different from its bottled equivalent, it will also taste slightly different each time you make it, which is the beauty of home cooking. So mix and match bought with homemade according to how much time you have and how you feel. It's a sensible, efficient and pleasurable way to cook good food, not only on a daily basis for yourself and maybe your family and friends, but also for special occasions.

IN THE STORECUPBOARD

STOCKING YOUR STORECUPBOARD with the items listed here will cut down on your regular shopping time because you will only need to buy fresh fish, meat, vegetables, eggs, dairy produce and fruit when you need them. All are used in the recipes in this book, so you will be able to turn your freshly bought produce into a superb meal in next to no time. Check the labels for storage times and to see whether bottles or jars need refrigerating once opened.

Bottles and Jars

Balsamic vinegar

Capers

Cider vinegar

Fish sauce (nam pla)

Honey

Malt vinegar (light)

Mayonnaise

Oil (sunflower, olive, nut and sesame)

Olive and tomato sauce

Olives (black and green)

Oyster sauce

Pesto (red and green)

Redcurrant jelly

Rice wine or sherry

Rice wine vinegar

Roasted peppers

Soy sauce

Sun-dried tomato paste (also in tubes)

Sun-dried tomatoes in olive oil

Tapenade (anchovy and olive paste)

Tomato ketchup

Wine vinegar (red, white and raspberry)

Worcestershire sauce

Cans

Anchovies

Chickpeas

Clams (also in jars)

Coconut milk

Consommé (chicken and beef)

Fish stock

Red kidney beans

Sweetcorn (plain, with sweet peppers and baby corn)

Tomatoes (whole and chopped)

Tomato purée (also in tubes)

Tuna

Dry Goods

Chocolate (good-quality white and dark)

Cocoa powder

Cornflour

Couscous (quick-cooking)

Flour

Gelatine (powdered)

Lentils

Noodles (oriental)

Nuts

Pasta (long and short)

Polenta (instant)

Raisins or currants

Rice (long grain, short grain risotto, basmati and Thai)

Stock cubes

Sugar (caster, demerara, granulated, icing and soft brown)

Trifle sponges or sponge fingers

Hot Flavourings

Chillies (crushed and whole dried red)

Green peppercorns in brine

Harissa (Tunisian hot chilli paste)

Mustard (Dijon, English powdered and wholegrain)

Thai curry paste (red and green)

Wasabi (Japanese horseradish paste)

Dried Herbs

Bay leaves

Herbes de Provence

Marjoram

Oregano

Rosemary

Thyme

Spices and Seasonings

Cardamom pods

Cayenne pepper

Chilli powder

Cinnamon (ground and sticks)

Coriander (ground and seeds)

Cumin (ground)

Curry powder

Five-spice powder

Garam masala

Ginger (ground)

Juniper berries

Mixed spice (ground)

Nutmeg (whole)

Paprika

Peppercorns (black, white and mixed colours)

Saffron (threads or powder)

Sea salt

Sesame seeds

Star anise

Bouquet Garni

This is a small herb 'packet' used to flavour foods cooked in liquid – especially soups, casseroles and stews. There are many good commercial brands available, both fresh and dried, but a bouquet garni is very easy to make yourself. The traditional combination is 1 bay leaf, 1 thyme sprig, a few parsley stalks and a celery leaf wrapped together in the green part of a leek and tied with kitchen string. If using dried herbs, wrap them in a small square of muslin rather than the leek.

Dry Rubs

These ground spices and flavourings are mixed together and rubbed over fish, poultry or meat before grilling or roasting. The basic mixtures can be used on their own, or you can add one or more of the optional ingredients.

Basic spice rub	Persian spice rub
cayenne	anise
garlic powder	cardamom
paprika	cinnamon
salt	coriander
	cumin
Optional extras	ginger
celery salt	mace
coriander	
cumin	
dried basil	
dried oregano	
dried sage	
ginger	
ground black pepper	
turmeric	

In the refrigerator

Aside from obvious ingredients you will regularly buy, like butter, cream, cheese and eggs, there are several invaluable homemade items you can store in the refrigerator – or freezer if you have one.

Roasted Garlic

whole heads of garlic
coarse sea salt (optional)
good-quality olive oil

1   Preheat the oven to 180°C (350°F) Gas 4. Place whole heads of garlic on a baking sheet or bed of coarse sea salt and roast in the oven for 30 minutes. Allow to cool, then cut off the top third of each head of garlic and squeeze the flesh out of the skins. Use the flesh straight away, or put it in a sterilized airtight jar, cover with olive oil and seal the jar. The garlic can be kept in the refrigerator for several weeks.

Roasted Peppers

whole peppers
good-quality olive oil

1   Preheat the oven to 190°C (375°F) Gas 5. Put the peppers in a roasting tin and roast for 40-50 minutes until the skins are charred and blistered on all sides. Turn the peppers several times during roasting.

2   Remove the roasted peppers from the oven and immediately place them in a plastic bag. Seal and leave to cool.

3   When the peppers are cold, peel off the skins and remove the cores and seeds. Pat the peppers dry and place in a sterilized airtight jar. Cover with olive oil and seal the jar. The peppers can be kept in the refrigerator for several weeks.

Basil Pesto

For a different flavour, replace about half the basil with flat-leaf parsley and the pine nuts with walnuts.

3 garlic cloves
90 g (3 oz) Parmesan cheese
60 g (2 oz) fresh basil leaves
60 g (2 oz) toasted pine nuts
100 ml (3½ fl oz) good-quality olive oil
salt and freshly ground black pepper

1   Roughly chop the garlic and grate the Parmesan cheese. Place in a food processor with the remaining ingredients and work to a purée. Taste for seasoning.

2   Use the pesto fresh or transfer to a sterilized airtight jar, cover with a thin film of olive oil and seal the jar. Store in the refrigerator for up to 1 week, or in the freezer for up to 1 month.

Red Pesto

60 g (2 oz) toasted pine nuts
60 g (2 oz) freshly grated Parmesan cheese
125 g (4 oz) well-drained sun-dried tomatoes in oil
100 ml (3½ fl oz) good-quality olive oil

1   Put the pine nuts, Parmesan and tomatoes in a food processor. Work to a purée, adding the oil through the feeder tube.

2   Use the pesto fresh or transfer to a sterilized airtight jar, cover with a thin film of olive oil and seal the jar. Store in the refrigerator for up to 1 week, or in the freezer for up to 1 month.

Basil Coulis

This sauce is good tossed with pasta or served with cold meats or hot fish.

1 large bunch of fresh basil
salt and freshly ground black pepper
200 ml (7 fl oz) good-quality olive oil
a few drops of lemon juice (optional)

1   Wash the basil and remove the leaves from the stalks. Discard the stalks. Dry the leaves on kitchen paper, then place them in a food processor with salt and pepper to taste.

2   With the machine running, add the olive oil through the feeder tube in a thin steady stream until the basil liquefies and is smooth. Add a few drops of lemon juice if you like the flavour with basil. Store in a sterilized airtight jar in the refrigerator for up to 1 week.

Moroccan Pickled Lemons

unwaxed lemons
granulated sugar
coarse sea salt

1   Blanch whole lemons in boiling water for 2-3 minutes. Drain and plunge immediately into cold water. Cut the lemons into quarters and remove any pips. Toss in granulated sugar until well coated.

2   Sprinkle the bottom of a sterilized airtight jar with coarse sea salt. Layer the lemon quarters in the jar, sprinkling coarse salt between the layers and pressing them down well to extract some juice. Seal and leave in a cold place for at least 15 days. Rinse before using.

Thai Green Curry Paste

For a really hot curry paste, leave the seeds in the chilli. The Thais always do.

3 garlic cloves
60 g (2 oz) fresh root ginger
2 lemon grass stalks
1 small green chilli
1 large handful of fresh coriander
1 tablespoon groundnut oil
salt and freshly ground black pepper

1   Peel the garlic and ginger and cut into large pieces. Roughly chop the lemon grass. Halve the chilli. Put all the ingredients in a food processor fitted with the metal blade and work to a paste. Store in a sterilized airtight jar in the refrigerator for up to 1 week or in the freezer for up to 1 month.

Mediterranean Marinade

Use for chicken and lamb. If fresh oregano is not available, use 1 teaspoon dried oregano.

4 tablespoons lemon juice
125 ml (4 fl oz) olive oil
2 teaspoons chopped fresh oregano
2 tablespoons chopped fresh basil
salt and freshly ground black pepper

1   Whisk together all the ingredients, adding salt and pepper to taste.

Teriyaki Marinade

Use for fish, chicken and meat. Minimum marinating time is 30 minutes; a few hours is ideal.

250 ml (8 fl oz) soy sauce
4 tablespoons rice wine vinegar
2–3 tablespoons caster sugar or runny honey
grated fresh root ginger, to taste
crushed garlic cloves, to taste

1   Whisk together all the ingredients. To use as a basting glaze, boil to reduce until syrupy.

Spiced Yogurt Marinade

Use for chicken and lamb.

300 ml (½ pint) natural yogurt
1 tablespoon mild curry paste
1 teaspoon cumin seeds
1 teaspoon black mustard seeds
1 tablespoon groundnut oil
salt and freshly ground black pepper

1   Whisk together all the ingredients, adding salt and pepper to taste.

Garlic Butter

For fish, poultry, meat and vegetables.

125 g (4 oz) garlic cloves
salt and freshly ground black pepper
125 g (4 oz) butter, softened

1   Peel the garlic, cut each clove in half and remove the green germ from the centre. Blanch the garlic cloves in salted boiling water for 3-4 minutes until just soft. Drain and leave to cool.

2   Press the garlic flesh through a sieve and mix with the butter and salt and pepper to taste. Wrap or cover tightly and store in the refrigerator for up to 1 week or in the freezer for up to 1 month.

Roasted Red Pepper Butter

For pasta, fish and chicken. If you like garlic, process 4-5 roasted garlic cloves with the peppers and butter.

100 g (3½ oz) well-drained roasted peppers in oil
150 g (5 oz) butter, softened
salt and freshly ground black pepper

1   Process the peppers and butter until smooth. Press through a sieve to remove any pieces of skin. Season to taste. Wrap or cover tightly and store in the refrigerator for up to 1 week or in the freezer for up to 1 month.

In the freezer

These items are useful to have in the freezer:

Homemade pesto and curry paste; crêpes; filo pastry; puff pastry; shortcrust pastry; peas and petits pois; prawns; root ginger (grate from frozen); lemon grass and ice-cream.

Nut Butter

For fish and vegetables.

100 g (3½ oz) shelled almonds or pistachio nuts
125 g (4 oz) butter, softened
salt and freshly ground black pepper

1   Crush or process the nuts with a few drops of water to make a fine paste. Mix with the butter and season to taste. Wrap tightly and store in the refrigerator for up to 1 week or in the freezer for up to 1 month.

Maître d'Hôtel Butter

For pasta, meat and vegetables.

100 g (3½ oz) butter, softened
1 tablespoon finely chopped fresh parsley
salt and freshly ground black pepper

1   Beat the butter until pale and fluffy. Mix in the parsley and salt and pepper to taste. Wrap or cover tightly and store in the refrigerator for up to 1 week or in the freezer for up to 1 month.

Snail Butter

For snails, pasta, meat and vegetables.

1 shallot
1 garlic clove
100 g (3½ oz) butter, softened
1 tablespoon finely chopped fresh parsley
salt and freshly ground black pepper

1   Chop the shallot and garlic very finely. Beat the butter until pale and fluffy. Mix in the chopped shallot, garlic, parsley and salt and pepper to taste. Wrap or cover tightly and store in the refrigerator for up to 1 week or in the freezer for up to 1 month.

Vinaigrette

The flavour of your vinaigrette will depend on the type of vinegar and oil used. Red wine vinegar is classic, sherry vinegar is slightly stronger, cider vinegar is mild. A neutral oil such as sunflower is good, but you may prefer the stronger flavour of olive oil, which can be fruity or peppery. Hazelnut and walnut oils are very strong in flavour, and best used in small quantities in combination with a light-flavoured oil such as sunflower.

Basic Vinaigrette

Plain vinaigrette dressing can be kept in a screw-top jar in the refrigerator for several weeks; dressings which contain herbs, shallots or garlic will only keep for 1 week.

1 part vinegar
salt and freshly ground black pepper
2–4 parts oil

1 Whisk the vinegar with salt and pepper to taste, then whisk in oil until both the flavour and consistency are to your liking.

Balsamic Vinaigrette

1 garlic clove
1 tablespoon balsamic vinegar
salt and freshly ground black pepper
2 tablespoons olive oil
4 tablespoons sunflower oil

1 Finely chop the garlic. Whisk the vinegar with the garlic and salt and pepper to taste, then whisk in both kinds of oil until thick.

Mustard Vinaigrette

2–3 teaspoons Dijon mustard
salt and freshly ground black pepper
2 tablespoons red wine vinegar
6 tablespoons olive oil

1 Put 2 teaspoons mustard in a bowl and add salt and pepper to taste. Mix well, then whisk in the vinegar. Gradually whisk in the oil until thick. Taste and add more mustard if you like.

Curry Lime Vinaigrette

finely grated rind of 3 limes
4 tablespoons lime juice
4 tablespoons mild curry powder or paste
125 ml (4 fl oz) groundnut oil
salt and freshly ground black pepper

1 Whisk all the ingredients together until evenly mixed, then taste for seasoning.

MAYONNAISE

THE TYPE OF oil you use depends on whether you want a light mayonnaise or one with more colour and flavour. Sunflower oil makes a mild mayonnaise, whereas extra-virgin olive oil can be quite fruity, strong and peppery. A mixture of the two is a happy compromise.

Because it contains raw egg, mayonnaise should be eaten within 2 days of making. Cover the surface of the mayonnaise with cling film and store in the refrigerator until ready to serve.

By hand

1 egg yolk
2 tablespoons Dijon mustard
salt and freshly ground black pepper
150–200 ml (5–7 fl oz) oil
juice of 1 lemon, or to taste

1   Whisk the egg yolk, mustard and salt and pepper in a bowl until well mixed and the salt has dissolved. Whisk in the oil a drop at a time until the mixture begins to emulsify, then whisk in a thin steady stream until the mayonnaise is thick. Add lemon juice to taste.

In the food processor

1 whole egg
2 tablespoons Dijon mustard
salt and freshly ground black pepper
150–200 ml (5–7 fl oz) oil
juice of 1 lemon, or to taste

1   Put the egg, mustard and salt and pepper in the bowl of a food processor and pulse to mix. With the machine running, add the oil through the feeder tube in a thin steady stream. Add lemon juice to taste.

Aïoli

This garlic mayonnaise from Provence is good with egg and fish dishes, and as a dip for crudités. Covered tightly with cling film, it will keep in the refrigerator for up to 2 days.

4 garlic cloves
salt and freshly ground black pepper
1 egg yolk
300 ml (½ pint) olive oil
a few drops of lemon juice, to taste

1   In a mortar, pound the garlic and ½ teaspoon salt to a paste with a pestle.

2   Add the egg yolk and whisk it in until evenly mixed, then add the oil a drop at a time, whisking vigorously until the mixture starts to emulsify.

3   Continue adding the oil gradually, whisking it in with a balloon whisk until all is incorporated and the aïoli is very thick. Add lemon juice and salt and freshly ground black pepper to taste.

Mayonnaise Variations

Sun-dried Tomato: Add 2 chopped sun-dried tomatoes in oil to the egg and seasoning mixture.

Lemon: Add the finely grated rind of 1 lemon to the egg and seasoning mixture.

Sweet Shortcrust Pastry

This rich dough, called pâte sucrée in French, is ideal for all sweet tarts. The quantity here is enough to line two 24.5 cm (9½ inch) tart tins. If not using it all, the remainder can be stored in the freezer for up to 1 month. To bake blind, see the method on page 163.

300 g (10 oz) plain flour
150 g (5 oz) chilled butter
60 g (2 oz) icing or caster sugar
1 medium egg
1 medium egg yolk
¾ teaspoon vanilla extract

1   Put the flour in a food processor. Cut the butter into 1.25 cm (½ inch) cubes and add to the flour. Process until the mixture looks like breadcrumbs. Add the sugar and pulse once to mix.

2   Mix the egg, egg yolk and vanilla extract. With the machine running, add the egg mixture and process until a rough dough forms.

3   Turn the dough out onto a work surface and form into 2 balls. Flatten both slightly and wrap in cling film. Chill 1 ball in the refrigerator for at least 30 minutes. Freeze the other.

4   To line a tart tin, roughly roll the chilled dough out on a floured surface with a floured rolling pin, then press it into the tin with your fingertips.

Crêpes

This recipe makes twelve 15-18 cm (6-7 inch) crêpes. The batter can be made in a food processor but it will need to be sieved before using, to remove any lumps.

100 g (3½ oz) plain flour
15 g (½ oz) caster sugar
pinch of salt
2 large eggs
300 ml (½ pint) milk
1 teaspoon vanilla extract
sunflower oil

1   Mix the flour, sugar and salt together in a bowl. Make a well in the centre and add the eggs. Mix the eggs with a balloon whisk, gradually drawing in the flour. Continue whisking and gradually add the milk until all is incorporated. Whisk in the vanilla extract and 2 teaspoons oil.

2   Heat a non-stick omelette or frying pan until very hot. Dip a wad of kitchen paper in oil, then wipe over the pan and heat until very hot. Whisk the batter well, then ladle a few tablespoonfuls into the pan and swirl around to coat the base. Cook for 1 minute or until golden underneath, then flip the crêpe over and cook for 30-60 seconds on the other side. Slide onto a plate.

3   Repeat with the remaining batter to make 12 crêpes, stacking them on top of one another and coating the pan with oil as necessary.

Index

Page numbers in *italics* refer to the illustrations